Meeting Rudolf Steiner

Selected and Introduced by Joan Almon
Series Editor: Robert McDermott

CLASSICS FROM

Journal for
ANTHROPOSOPHY

NUMBER 75   FALL 2005

This volume is a series of "classical" articles from the following issues of the
Journal for Anthroposophy: Walter, Spring 1967; Schweitzer, Fall 1966;
Belyi, Spring 1977, Fall 1977, Spring 1978, and Fall 1980;
Clark and Eaton, Fall 1971; Monges, Spring 1979;
Ege, Spring 1969 and Fall 1974.

We extend thanks to the Rudolf Steiner Archive (*Nachlassverwaltung*) and to
the Goetheanum, both in Dornach, Switzerland, for use of their photographs.
Photo credits: Back cover, O. Rietmann;
Head of Christ, page 89, Thomas Spalinger. Others are unknown.

Front cover and layout: Seiko Semones

Published by the
Anthroposophical Society in America

Journal for Anthroposophy
1923 Geddes Avenue
Ann Arbor, MI 48104

ISSN-0021-8235

Printed by McNaughton & Gunn, Inc., Saline, Michigan

CONTENTS

FOREWORD

Robert McDermott
Series Editor

This slim but significant volume rescues from early issues of the *Journal for Anthroposophy* writings on the individuality and influence of Rudolf Steiner. With an introduction by Joan Almon, co-general secretary of the Anthroposophical Society, these writings are here reprinted in order to allow readers in the early 21st century to meet Rudolf Steiner through memoirs written by those who knew him.

The *Journal for Anthroposophy* began publishing in 1963 under the editorship of Henry Barnes, for many years the general secretary of the Anthroposophical Society, and in subsequent years in turn by Christy MacKaye Barnes, Arthur Zajonc, Hilmar and Claire Moore, and Sherry Wildfeuer on behalf of the Collegium of the School of Spiritual Science.

As part of the decision of the council of the Anthroposophical Society in America to suspend publication of the *Journal* in 2002 while the council reviewed the Society's publication program, it was agreed that I would serve as general editor for a series of volumes of selections, or "classics," from early issues of the *Journal*.

This volume, *Meeting Rudolf Steiner*, will be followed by three additional volumes on subjects such as:

> *Imagination*, edited and introduced by Kate Farrell,
> *Science*, edited and introduced by Arthur Zajonc,
> *Culture*, edited and introduced by Douglas Sloan.

These four volumes will be published over the next two years by the Anthroposophical Society and distributed by SteinerBooks.

Introduction
Classics from the Journal for Anthroposophy

Joan Almon

This volume of the Classics series of the *Journal for Anthroposophy* focuses on Rudolf Steiner in a very direct way through the memories of those who knew him. These authors share with us rich experiences and warm insights about the man and his work, especially some of the highpoints of his life – the way he guided the building of the first Goetheanum, for instance, and how he responded to the terrible fire that destroyed it. What emerges from their writings is a portrait of a man of great courage, and of warmth and of humor, whose mission was to help humanity develop a new science of the spirit. He shared a profound understanding of the spiritual world and how such an understanding could be developed to bring about renewal in many spheres of life, including meditative work, the arts and sciences, education, agriculture, and medicine. Through his spiritual teaching and esoteric research called Anthroposophy and the founding of the Anthroposophical Society he developed an approach that has been applied by many thousands of individuals, in many cultures, and in many diverse spheres of life. It continues to grow and expand and has touched the lives of hundreds of thousands — perhaps millions — of individuals around the world.

It is hard to understand an individuality who was able to work so deeply and in so many fields. He was well-educated in both the sciences and the humanities. He studied at the Technical University in Vienna, and received a doctorate in philosophy from the University of Rostock. His inner training was of equal importance. Some of the indications he gave concerning his own inner development are found in selections in this volume. His lifework was incredibly rich. He wrote over 20 books, delivered 6000 lectures in more than a dozen European countries, developed new art forms, helped establish Waldorf schools, Biodynamic farms, curative communities and much more. This volume does not attempt to be a biography. There are many biographies that look at the fullness of Steiner's life in a much more complete way. There are a few incidents in Steiner's early life, however, that stand out as being very significant for his overall development. They are included here as another picture that helps us to understand this remarkable individual.

Steiner's family is often described in humble terms as a working class family. This is outwardly true, but it is also true that his father was educated by monks and even given funds for beginning his studies in a Gymnasium, an academic high school from which a graduate could enter a university. Steiner's father was not able to take advantage of this opportunity, but he did take a serious interest in his son's education, directing him toward the study of science and technology, rather than humanities which Steiner himself might have chosen.

Steiner's father, Johann Steiner, was born in 1829 and died in 1910; his mother Franziska Blie, was born in 1834 and died on Christmas Eve, 1918. A photograph of her portrays a modest woman with a very sensitive and beautiful face. The future parents of Rudolf Steiner met while working on an estate in the Waldviertel, a forested, rural section of Austria. They sought permission to marry from Count Hoyos, for whom they worked, but could not receive his permission to do so. Finally they left his estate and married on May 16, 1860. Johann Steiner then took up work as a telegraph operator with the Austrian railroad and later became a stationmaster in charge of small stations south of Vienna. Within a year he was assigned to work at the station in Kraljevak, on the eastern border of Austria in the former Yugoslavia. In late February 1861, Rudolf Steiner was born there, just nine months after his parents married.[1]

The changes in his parents' new circumstances had several great consequences for his life. Because he was born on the eastern border of Austria and then spent his childhood years growing up in railroad stations within a few hours of Vienna, he grew up straddling the boundaries of eastern and western Europe, experiencing the influences of both. Living near Vienna also meant being part of a much more artistic and cosmopolitan environment than he would have experienced had his parents remained in the more provincial Waldviertel. It is also noteworthy that he spent his childhood years growing up beside the railroad stations of the 1860s and '70s, when railroads were at the leading edge of technological development. Such an upbringing was the equivalent of growing up today in Silicon Valley.

Steiner remained close to his family throughout his life. His letters to them are particularly warm and show a side of his nature not readily visible in his books and lectures which generally have a very formal tone. After his father's death he made financial contributions to his family and shortly before his death Steiner wrote to Marie Steiner expressing concern for the financial well-being of his sister, Leopoldine, who was growing blind.[2] Leopoldine Steiner was born in 1864 and died in 1927. She was a dressmaker and lived with her family for her entire life. Rudolf Steiner's brother Gustav was born in 1866 and died in 1941. He was born deaf and did not develop an ability to speak, thus needing special help all through his life. His brother's experience may have had a profound influence on Rudolf Steiner's development of curative education later in his life.

Steiner's childhood seems to have been blessed with loving and caring parents, but their financial circumstances were extremely modest. He describes this aspect of his childhood himself, although in the third person:

> "The family always had to struggle with conditions which, in keeping with the situation of that time, can only be described as a 'fight against the low wages of a lesser railway official'. His parents — this must be emphasized to avoid misunderstandings — were always ready to sacrifice their last penny for their children's welfare; but not many such 'last pennies' were available."[3]

Rudolf Steiner does not say much about the spiritual aspects of his childhood, but he does describe in detail one experience which had a very profound effect on him. He tells of sitting alone in the waiting room of the small station where he and his family lived, and speaks of himself in the third person.

> "As he was sitting there, the door opened. He found it quite natural that a person came through the door, a woman he had never seen before but who closely resembled a member of the family. She entered the door, went to the middle of the room, made some gestures and also

spoke words that could be rendered as follows: 'Try now and later to do for me as much as you can'. She remained in the room for a while and made gestures that can never vanish from the soul that has once seen them; then she went to the stove and disappeared into it."

"The impression left upon the boy by this event was a very strong one. The boy had no one in the family to whom he could have spoken about this, and if he had spoken of it, he would already at that time have been scolded severely for his foolish superstition. Soon after this event, the following occurred. His father, who was ordinarily a very cheerful man, grew very sad after that day, and the boy could see that his father did not wish to talk about something that he knew. A few days later, ... the following news leaked out. In a place that was situated quite far from the station, a close family relation committed suicide at the very hour in which the small boy had seen the figure in the waiting room. The boy had never seen that relative, nor had he heard much about her. ... The event made a strong impression on him, for it was undoubtedly the spirit of the woman who had committed suicide who had approached the boy, asking him to help her in the time following death."

"... from that event onward a life in the boy's soul began to develop which thoroughly revealed to him the worlds out of which not only the outer trees, the outer mountains, speak to the human soul but also the worlds that are behind them. From that point in time onward, the boy lived with the spirits of nature, which can be observed quite particularly in such a region; he lived with the creative beings behind things, and he allowed them to work upon him in the same way as he allowed the outer world to work upon him."[4]

One can trace at least two major themes of Rudolf Steiner's work from this moment in his childhood. Repeatedly during his life he devoted himself to a concern for how the living might serve the dead, and how the dead continue to care about and serve the living. He gave many verses that can be recited by those on earth for those in the spiritual world.[5] Recitation of these verses can help to deepen the relationship between the living and the dead. He also suggested reading to the dead. For Steiner, the veil between the spiritual world and the earthly world is thin and protective, not a dense curtain or a heavy wall separating the two. The transition from one world to the other was just that — a transition, a movement between different but complementary worlds.

Uncovering the secrets of nature proved to be a second theme in which Steiner sustained a lifelong interest. This relationship between higher worlds and the world of nature was a powerful motif throughout his life and enabled him to develop an approach to nature that can lead to an understanding of the spiritual beings at work in the shaping and forming of the earth and its elements. This deep interest led Steiner to develop the foundation for Biodynamic agriculture and for what is called Goethean science, an approach to understanding nature based on observation and a deep imaginative relationship with whatever is being observed.

For Steiner, this childhood experience of his deceased relative helped to indicate his clairvoyant perception of spiritual realities. It is not unusual for children to have perceptions of the spiritual world. Such perceptions ordinarily fade as children grow older. In Steiner's case, he was able to keep these experiences alive. He was aided in this by a series of meetings with individuals very important to his destiny. One of these was Felix Koguzki, an herb gatherer who took the train each week to Vienna to sell his herbs to pharmacies. He traveled on the same train that Steiner took daily to attend the University and they developed a very close personal and esoteric relationship. Of him, Rudolf Steiner says:

> "We became friends, and it was possible to speak of the spiritual world with him as someone of experience. He was deeply pious and uneducated in the usual sense of the word. True, he had read many books on mysticism, but what he said certainly was not influenced by such reading. Rather, it flowed from a soul life that bore within it a very elemental creative wisdom. … With him one could look deeply into the secrets of nature. … One could 'learn' nothing from this man in the usual sense of the word. But through him, and with one's own powers of perceptions of the spiritual world, one could gain significant glimpses into that world where this man had a firm footing."[6]

Later, Steiner experienced a great teacher whom he refers to as the Master. In one place he says, "I did not meet the M. [the Master] immediately, but first an emissary who was completely initiated into the secrets of the plants and their effects, and into their connections with the cosmos and human nature. Contact with the spirits of nature was something self-evident for him, about which he talked without enthusiasm; but he aroused enthusiasm all the more."7 It would certainly seem that he is speaking here of the herb gatherer, Felix, whom he later included in his mystery dramas as the wise woodsman, Felix Balde.

These are just a few moments out of the richness of Rudolf Steiner's early life which can serve as a background to the accounts in this Journal of his later years. When one studies his adult years there is a certain pattern that emerges. While he often spoke of the threefold nature of the human being which included thinking (or spiritual forces), feeling (or artistic forces), and willing (or world of activity), it was also the case that he lived intensively into each of these realms of activity at different points in his own life.

From his student years until around 1910 he devoted himself to putting forth his philosophical perspective, particularly his systematic epistemology. His basic books were written during these years and from them one gets a broad picture of Steiner's understanding of the universe, of the human being, and of a contemporary spiritual path for individuals who wish to attain a knowledge of higher worlds that can be applied in daily life for the transformation of self and of the world.

This work on philosophy and spiritual activity continued through his whole life, but from 1910, when he wrote his first mystery drama, through the years of the first World War, when he built the first Goetheanum, he also worked intensively on the renewal of the arts. In relationship to the design and building of the remarkable double-domed Goetheanum, he entered deeply into sculpture, designing the pillars and the spaces between them so that the walls had a living, sculptural nature. He also worked with Edith Maryon on the 30-foot-high sculpture, called "The Representative of Humanity," of which it has been said that the whole of Anthroposophy can be found.

In this statue, the Christ is the central figure, and with his outstretched hands He holds in place the two beings of temptation. Ahriman in his cave seeks to chain humanity to the earth through rank materialism, while Lucifer, the fallen angel, seeks to inspire humanity with a spirituality that divorces humanity from the earth. The great guiding figure of humanity, the Christ, reaches one arm up and the other down, protecting humanity from Ahriman and Lucifer who would tempt us from the middle path. Rudolf Steiner described the Christ as bringing the force of love to the Earth and one feels He is using love to hold them in their rightful places.

The Greeks spoke of this cosmic being as the Logos, or the Word, and the Gospel of John describes how the Logos entered into the physical body and became flesh. According to Rudolf Steiner this took place when Jesus was baptized in the River Jordan. He became anointed, or filled, with the Christ Being. *Christos* in Greek means anointed. After the Baptism Jesus lived for three years, and became the vessel through which the Christ dwelled on the earth. It is these years which are described in the New Testament.

Equally moving are Steiner's descriptions of this Being today, for he says that after the crucifixion and resurrection the Christ returned to the cosmos, journeying through the cosmic spheres as does the human soul after death. Since the 20th century Christ has returned to the sphere of the earth, living in the etheric or life body of the earth. In this new state he is experienced by many, Christians and non-Christians, who respond to the force of love which is characteristic of the Christ. One can have direct experiences of the Christ today, whether one is fully prepared or not, but one can also be on a path of inner striving to reach the etheric world which is now penetrated by the Christ. There are many paths to the Christ, and one can view Anthroposophy with its emphasis on spiritual study, meditative activity, artistic experiences and practical work penetrated by spiritual insight in a host of fields as a preparation or initiation for meetings with the Christ.

It is hard to know what to call this Being today. Christ, meaning 'anointed', was the appropriate name 2000 years ago when Jesus was anointed in the River Jordan. Representative of Humanity was one name that Rudolf Steiner used to describe this great Being. Some people prefer Spirit of Humanity. In the Foundation Stone Mantra which Steiner gave during the Christmas Foundation Meeting in 1923, he devotes the fourth and final panel to the Christ. Here he speaks of the quality of light again and again, but the closest he comes to using a name is "Light Divine, Christ Sun." In my mind, the fourth panel and the statue of the Representative of Humanity go together. They both portray the Spirit of Humanity today, filled with light and love, yet engaged in a great battle to create a safe space in which the human being can grow into his or her own destiny.

Artists carried out Steiner's designs for painting the ceiling of the Goetheanum using vibrant natural colors which he helped develop. He gave sketches and inspiration to the artists who carved the glass windows for the Goetheanum. As accounts in this volume indicate, he was deeply engaged in all aspects, practical and artistic, of the building process.

He also brought renewal to speech and movement, working closely with Marie Steiner to develop the drama and speech work, as well as eurythmy in which speech and music are made visible through movement. The stage of the Goetheanum was intended to showcase these new arts. All of these arts were intensively developed during the war years when artists from warring nations worked together on the first Goetheanum.

Toward the end of the war and in the years immediately following it, Rudolf Steiner turned his attention to what is sometimes called the highest art — the social art. He worked extensively on his ideas about the threefold social order and attempted to bring them into practice in post-war Europe where so many social changes were taking place. The Threefold Social Order focuses on how society can be organized according to three great principles: that the realm of law be governed by a concern for the rights of citizens and a recognition of the equality of all human beings; that the cultural life, which embraces religion, education and the arts, recognize the unique nature of each human being; and that the economic realm be developed in ways that recognize a cooperative spirit of brotherhood and sisterhood.

Unfortunately, the application of these social ideas was probably the area of his work where he met with the greatest resistance and the least success. Granted, he did not expect full success until far in the future, but he clearly hoped that these ideas could at least begin to take hold in post-war Europe and elsewhere. These ideas have not been lost, however, and there are many who work with them today in the hope that they can become the guiding principles of societies in the future.

The third area of Steiner's work, and the most visible in the world today, are the practical works that he developed in the last period of his life, from around 1919 until his death in 1925. This is the period during which he created Waldorf schools, curative homes, medical practices, Biodynamic farms, and more. These institutions or initiatives (as they are sometimes called), have grown enormously in the past 85 years. It is now estimated that there are about 10,000 of them in the world, each independent but generally working together freely in associations.

Today, these three legacies of Rudolf Steiner — philosophical-spiritual, artistic, and practical initiatives — are interwoven within the Anthroposophical Society. Within this Society there is a central core, the School of Spiritual Science, whose purpose is to further research in all these areas. This enables the insights of Rudolf Steiner to remain alive and to grow in ways appropriate to our times. Were it not for the existence of the Society, Rudolf Steiner's gifts to the world would probably remain separate from each other with little to link them together. They would be like individual organs that have not found a way to collaborate and strengthen each other within a single body. Fortunately, Rudolf Steiner took a major step in weaving his legacy of insight and practical work together a year before his death when he refounded the Anthroposophical Society at Christmas 1923 during the Christmas Foundation Conference. This founding conference, an amazing spiritual event, is vividly described in this volume.

From one point of view, Rudolf Steiner did not name a successor to carry on his work. This is true in the usual sense of 'successor', but from a different perspective one can say that the Anthroposophical Society itself serves as his successor. The Society is a summation of all that he developed in his lifetime and a foundation for all that can come next. It was created in 1923 and survived a serious split, World War II, and the closing of the Society and Waldorf schools under both Nazism and Communism. Although the challenges of the 21st century are different from those of the 20th, the Society is again deeply challenged to serve humanity during a difficult time. On the one hand, many human beings are at a threshold where they are waking up to their own soul-spiritual nature which they are seeking to understand. At the same time, the forces of materialism, which oppose this development are growing stronger than ever and create many barriers for children and adults to achieve their spiritual potential. In Rudolf Steiner's lifework we find deep insights into this current situation, and we find indications for meeting these challenges with a courageous spirit. Rudolf Steiner identifies this spirit with the Archangel Michael.

The authors of the articles in this *Journal* had the opportunity of experiencing Rudolf Steiner firsthand. Their lives were changed by these meetings and their gratitude is apparent. Through these articles, the man Rudolf Steiner and the enormous task he undertook in his lifetime becomes more visible and tangible.

In the essay by Bruno Walter we see how a great musician was deeply moved by his meeting with Rudolf Steiner and by his study of Anthroposophy. The renowned humanitarian, Albert Schweitzer, was also stirred by his meeting with Rudolf Steiner. Although Schweitzer chose not to pursue Anthroposophy, from his letter to Bruno Walter one sees how throughout his life he treasured his meeting with Steiner. There are also articles by individuals well-known in anthroposophic circles — the poet Arvia MacKaye Ege, eurythmist Lisa Monges, Sonia Tomara Clark and Jeannette Eaton. All of them describe their experiences of Rudolf Steiner, including some of the most intense moments of Steiner's life, such as the burning of the first Goetheanum and the Christmas Foundation Meeting.

A centerpiece of this volume is the excerpt from a book by Andrei Belyi, the Russian novelist and Symbolist poet. His descriptions of Steiner and their time together are written with the sensitive perceptions and rich language one would expect from such an artistic author, combined with the deep attention to soul life one often experiences among Russian people and in Russian literature. In a letter to his friend, Alexander Blok, another Russian Symbolist poet, Belyi describes his first meeting with Rudolf Steiner and mentions seeing Steiner's aura. He adds that he had been able to see auras for the previous year.[8] While this capacity is not mentioned in the articles in this issue, it perhaps plays a part in Belyi's extraordinary perceptiveness.

All of these articles have appeared in past issues of the *Journal for Anthroposophy*. Many subscribers have read them over a period of years, but not in as concentrated a form as they are presented here. The Council of the U.S. Anthroposophical Society felt it would be unfortunate to let these fine pieces fade from memory and be unavailable to newer readers. Thus came the decision to publish several issues of the *Journal* containing "classic" articles on several topics. This volume which focuses on the life of Rudolf Steiner is the first in that series. Future issues will focus on imagination, science and culture. Robert McDermott is the general editor of the series.

Rudolf Steiner, standing beside his younger sister, Leopoldine.

My Way to Anthroposophy
A Musician's Tribute to Rudolf Steiner

Bruno Walter

*This tribute was written by Bruno Walter — the world-famous conductor —
in 1960 as a contribution to a volume which was intended for publication in
honor of Rudolf Steiner's centennial in 1961. Unfortunately, the volume did
not appear and this essay was not published in English until it appeared in the*
Journal for Anthroposophy *in 1967. Originally written in English, Bruno
Walter rewrote it in German for publication in the weekly magazine,* Das
Goetheanum *(Vol. XL, No. 52, 1961) which was at that time edited by his
Swiss poet-friend, Albert Steffen.*

If after a long life in the service of music I feel called upon to join the
many voices from other fields of cultural life who pay tribute to Rudolf
Steiner and express their veneration for this great teacher of mankind and
his profound message, it is, aside from my admiration for the universality
of his genius, a very personal gratitude which strives for expression. For
just as his teachings shed light on almost all fields of human spiritual
endeavor, they also disclose the deepest meanings of music. As I have
already described, in my book on *Music and Music Making*,[9] I experienced
how Rudolf Steiner's ideas on music in their essentials confirmed what I
had thought and felt about my art, and what it had become for me
throughout the activity of a long life. So to my great satisfaction I received
from the lofty viewpoint of the spiritual investigator a seal of confirmation
upon my basic musical convictions as well as on my life as a musician.

Yet it was not as a musician that I found my way to Anthroposophy.
Having grown up in Germany, surrounded by German culture, I have
always considered myself a disciple of Goethe. From my earliest years, I
have felt a deep affinity with his Faust. An ardent longing for light and

knowledge dominated my inner life, and from my present viewpoint as an anthroposophist I believe I can discern in this thirst for knowledge, in my closeness to nature, and, above all, in my early religious leanings, the signs of my predisposition to Anthroposophy. Yet these unconscious capacities required many years for their development until, in my old age, I was able clearly to recognize Anthroposophy as my destiny.

In his lectures entitled "The Experience of Tone in Man", given for the teachers of the Waldorf School, Rudolf Steiner said: "To comprehend and experience music truly means to enter the world of the spirit." As a pupil of Rudolf Steiner's, I see in the way in which music flooded my soul from my earliest childhood on and in my lifelong dedication to my art, the manifestation of such spiritual presentiment within me. But destiny did not recompense my fervent strivings by affording me an early contact with spiritual science, or a personal acquaintance with Rudolf Steiner, for which my musical activities in Vienna and later in Munich would have offered ample opportunity. How decisively such an event could have shortened my way! But, as it was, I had to travel a long path into old age without the helpful intervention of destiny. Rudolf Steiner died in 1925, and I was seventy-two when, in 1948, I was introduced to the profound world conception of this enlightened and enlightening spirit. Then, the further I progressed in this field of knowledge, the more clearly I recognized that, without knowing it, my development had proceeded constantly in the direction of Anthroposophy. Since that time I have entrusted myself to the guidance of Rudolf Steiner and in so doing have experienced the rare happiness of becoming once again — old as I am — a "pupil."

It was really a new world which Steiner's insight opened up to me, a world, which, if I was to live in it, required a drastic change in my whole way of thinking. For many years I had lived under the influence of the philoso-phy of Kant and had accepted as final his verdict that human knowledge is confined to the sense world. Now I learned that it was possible for a highly intensified capacity of knowledge to win entrance to supersensible realms. From Rudolf Steiner's thought there now flowed unending light, illuminating cosmos, earth and man, the physical and spiritual worlds. It meant an immeasurable enrichment for someone of my age in this era of depressing materialism to feel firm ground under his feet at last in the certainty that everything material is the manifestation of the spiritual. Herein I recognized one of the fundamental premises of Anthroposophy and with a certain satisfaction I remembered that in my autobiography, Theme and Variations, written long before my contact with spiritual science, I had told of my youthful discovery "of the reality of the spiritual side of everything that exists."

Yet however certain I was of the reality of the spirit as the basis of Anthroposophy, I had to recognize that the universality of the thought world which Steiner revealed did not permit of any such simplification as a "basic principle." Soon I realized that only years of study could help me to find my way into these wide new spheres.

If I am not mistaken, my first adventure in this world was a study of Rudolf Steiner's *Philosophy of Thomas Aquinas.* Then followed *The Bhagavad Gita and the Epistles of St. Paul.* Prepared through these deep experiences, I devoted myself to the study of his comparatively early book, *Theosophy*, followed by his major works, *Occult Science: An Outline and How to Attain Knowledge of the Higher Worlds.* What enlightenment I received from the numerous cycles of lectures through which I gradually progressed and which, together with the study of his autobiography, *The Course of My Life*, confirmed me in my definite acceptance of Anthroposophy as my given path of life. From reading *The Course of My Life* there developed in me a relation of deep personal devotion to this great teacher of mankind, who took his readers along with him on his earthly pilgrimage towards the sublime experience of his Christological intuitions.

My approach to Steiner's encyclopedic work and my efforts to fathom his towering individuality, received valuable support from the personal records, *Meetings with Rudolf Steiner* by Albert Steffen and by Friedrich Rittelmeyer — and no less from the letters and poems of the great German poet, Christian Morgenstern — all of which evoked before me the heartwarming and, at the same time, awe-inspiring image of a seer, to whose vision the past and the future lay open and whose words shed light in both directions.

Rudolf Steiner, around 1900.

I went to Dornach in order to visit the place where Rudolf Steiner had lived and from which his teachings went out into the world. There I visited the poet and thinker Albert Steffen. Deep is my admiration for the poet's unique ethical and spiritual personality and for his untiring service to the work of his great friend. I felt, indeed, in everyone and everything, as in the whole atmosphere of the Goetheanum, the enduring influence of Rudolf Steiner's individuality. Dornach also offered me the unforgettable experience of a stage rehearsal of Albert Steffen's drama Barrabas, the author at my side, seated on a low step of the stalls, watching the progress of the Biblical play, the product of his creative genius. The public performance of the drama confirmed and strengthened the deep impression I had had in the rehearsal and I remembered Rudolf Steiner's word about the importance of the dramatic arts in the field of Anthroposophy.

In this connection I will also mention my first impression of eurythmy, for which the stage of the Goetheanum again proved to be the ideal setting. This new art, created by Rudolf Steiner's musical-visual inspiration, gave me a highly interesting experience: melody and musical rhythm — or the metric life of spoken verses — are here "translated" into the artistic language of an uplifting style of dance, grounded in the soul's experience, "translated" by means of the beautiful and expressive gestures and rhythmically moving figures of the eurythmists. Their eloquent perform-ance, singly or in groups, proved the rich potentialities and originality of this art. I shall not forget the stirring impression of the scene showing Odysseus' descent into Hades and his encounter with the shade of his mother. With the help of the very moving exposition of Ralph Kux' musical composition, it conjured up the magic of Homeric poesy from a timeless past.

In Dornach I also met Wilhelm Lewerenz, to whom the musical work at the Goetheanum was entrusted at that time. He was kind enough to acquaint me for the first time with remarks of Dr. Steiner on music, showing me, to my surprise, his deep insight into the innermost sense of music. In the course of time Wilhelm Lewerenz became a dear friend of mine. I love to think back to my later encounters with this high-minded personality in Vienna and Rome — but only a short time was granted our friendship for he soon had to leave this earth. Karl v. Baltz, outstanding violinist and true anthroposophist, became his successor. He has made a systematic study of Steiner's thoughts on music and he has had the great kindness, in compliance with my request, to let me know the result of these studies. It was with the warmest gratitude that I made use of his kind and unselfish communications which have enabled me to add, to the all-embracing veneration for Rudolf Steiner's work that fills my heart, the expression of my particular devotion as a musician.

Gradually it became clear to me that music is a vital power in the universe as Steiner reveals it. I do not even think it too audacious to assert that according to him the cosmos "sounds." He fully accepts the Pythagorean idea of "the harmonies of the spheres" and extends and deepens it. Besides, his heart is wide open to the power of musical melodies and harmonies and he recognizes in our great music, memories and premonitions of the wonder of existence in a higher world. May I quote what he said:

> "We can now understand wherein the deepest significance of music lies, why all who know the inner relationship of things concede to music the highest place among the arts, why music touches and makes the deepest strings in our soul resound. The higher world is man's original homestead and the echoes from this native world, the world of the spirit, resound for him in the harmonies and melodies of the physical world. They permeate this lower world with intimations of an existence filled with glory and wonder; they move his innermost being and thrill it with emotions of purest joy, of loftiest spirituality, such as this world cannot give him. Painting speaks to his astral, or sentient nature, but the world of music speaks to his very inner being. And as long as man is not yet an initiate, his home world, the world of spirit, is given him in music."

I found these revealing remarks on music in a lecture which Dr. Steiner held in Berlin in November 1906. From this lecture we learn at the same time how overwhelmingly the emotional power and the beauty of music filled Rudolf Steiner's own soul.

This natural and genuinely loving reaction to the emotional power of music can already be seen in Steiner's memories of his childhood described in *The Course of My Life*. There he tells how grateful he was to the assistant schoolteacher in the village of Neudoerfl, where the Steiner family lived. Rudolf was then a boy about eight years old and he owed to his teacher the introduction to the world of art as well as his first impressions of geometry. The teacher played the violin and piano, which "inwardly strongly attract-ed" the boy and often he could experience in the neighboring place of Sauerbrunn the deep impressions of Hungarian Gypsy music. I remember from my own experience the highly talented, passionate playing of the Gypsy musicians and I am sure that the lively impression of which Steiner still spoke after so many years reveals his genuinely musical soul as a child.

Truly enlightening are Dr. Steiner's thoughts about the musical intervals, his profound remarks about "major" and "minor" and other fundamental musical conceptions, and I feel that such ideas of his will be recognized one day as an important contribution to scientific musical theory of the future, just as numerous other perceptions of his ever-fertile mind in varied fields of spiritual endeavor will — for a long time to come — furnish thematic material for scientific elaboration and development.

During the last years of his life his great-hearted readiness to give of his spiritual insight enriched the medical, the agricultural, the pedagogical and other professions with revolutionary perceptions and he gladly imparted of his wisdom to all who asked for it.

In this connection, I would like to draw attention to the developments in the field of religion which grew out of the answers he was able to give to the young priests, under the leadership of Friedrich Rittelmeyer and Emil Bock, who had been deeply moved by his insight into the nature and destiny of Christ and came to Rudolf Steiner for advice and help. Personally I can only speak of the Christian Community with warmest gratitude. The friendship which I have been privileged to enjoy with Emil Bock, Rittelmeyer's successor as leader of The Christian Community, I count among the most valued gifts of destiny. His eloquent and illuminating observations on Christianity, based upon a profound acquaintance with the work of Rudolf Steiner, have enlightened my own study of spiritual science.

Dr. Steiner's innermost compassion for the needs of humanity and his love for his fellow human beings can be seen in the help he gave in response to the requests which came to him from persons representing the most varied fields of cultural endeavor, and he lives in the results which flow from the help he gave. Incalculable, for instance, are the practical benefits of his ped-agogical suggestions which have their origin in his knowledge of man and, in particular, of the child and the different stages of child development. I have made a point of studying Rudolf Steiner's numerous educational writings and have been especially impressed by the emphasis which he places on the role of artistic activities — including drawing, painting, music — in early childhood education and was particularly gratified to discover again in this realm the significance he attaches to music. The early introduction of artistic experience clearly shows Dr. Steiner's intention of first nourishing and educating the soul of the child before making demands upon his intellect, as well as his fundamental policy which aims not merely at imparting information but at the education of character. His pedagogical ideas mark the beginning of a new chapter in the art of education and the advantages they possess over customary methods employed in our schools justify our hopes in the future generations whose childhood and youth have been exposed to this beneficial influence. In this connection I should also like to mention Rudolf Steiner's loving concern for the fate of so-called "retarded children." There are now schools in many countries which apply Rudolf Steiner's principles to curative education with excellent results.

My personal gratitude as a musician to Rudolf Steiner includes his thoughts on education, the very spirit of which emanates from his lectures. For, in a sense, the activity of an opera or symphony conductor, to which so many years of my life have been devoted, is to a great extent also that of an educator. One of our main tasks is to guide artists, to develop their talents, to obtain and keep their good will, to raise their accomplishments — in short: to educate them. But beyond Rudolf Steiner's pedagogical vocation, I understand him as an *educator of humanity* in the highest sense of this high notion and I am sure that future generations will see him in this light. So my devotion for him is very different from that of a conductor or musical educator, for my musicianship means to me far more than mere musical activities such as performing, teaching or conducting; it means a soul filled with music, dominated by its supersensible power. It means a bridge to a higher world, and from that kind of musicianship flows my gratitude to Rudolf Steiner for his spiritual scientific confirmation of my being as a musician and for the profound significance he attributes to music in his conception of the world.

Nowhere is this expressed in a deeper and more essential way than in the prophetic passage in a lecture held in 1924 at Torquay, England, in which he says: "It may come about some day — whether or not this will happen depends entirely on man himself — that it will be just in the realm of music that the impulse of Christ in its true form will reveal itself before the world."

Notes Concerning Albert Schweitzer and Rudolf Steiner

Bruno Walter, the conductor, and Albert Schweitzer, the humanitarian, had been friends for many years. Among a wide range of common interests they shared was a deep admiration for the German poet and thinker, Goethe. Also, Walter knew that his friend Schweitzer had once met Rudolf Steiner and had not forgotten the impression left by this encounter. In 1960, Bruno Walter was most active in helping to plan and to prepare a fitting commemoration for the hundredth anniversary of Rudolf Steiner's birth which was to be celebrated the following year.

In considering who might be asked to contribute to this event, Bruno Walter offered to write Albert Schweitzer and invite him to take part. It was in response to his friend's request, that Albert Schweitzer wrote the recollections of his meeting with Rudolf Steiner which had occurred more than half a century before. Bruno Walter sent Schweitzer a number of Rudolf Steiner's books and hoped that his old friend might, in this way, have the opportunity to renew his contact with the spiritual teacher who had meanwhile come to occupy a position of such paramount importance in his own inner life during his later years. He was deeply pleased by Albert Schweitzer's response and treasured the letter which accompanied the reminiscences, part of which is reproduced below. Bruno Walter shared Schweitzer's reply with Albert Steffen, the friend of his later years, from whom he received a letter which throws light on Rudolf Steiner's interest in Albert Schweitzer and the hopes he had entertained of their meeting. The pertinent passage from this letter is also printed here in translation.

My Meeting with Rudolf Steiner

Albert Schweitzer

My meeting with Rudolf Steiner took place on the occasion of a Theosophical conference in Strasbourg. If I am not mistaken, it was either in 1902 or 1903. Annie Besant, with whom I had become acquainted through friends in Strasbourg, introduced us to each other. Rudolf Steiner entered at that time into connection with the Theosophical Society, not so much because he shared its convictions as because he expected the possibility of finding among its members those who would have interest and understanding for the spiritual truths which he had to present.

I knew that he had occupied himself in Weimar with the study of Goethe. He, quite naturally, knew nothing of the young instructor at the University of Strasbourg who had busied himself with Kant's philosophy and the problems of the historical investigation of the life of Jesus. He was, indeed, fourteen years older than I.

French was the language in which this meeting of theosophists was conducted. As I spoke German, they counted on my devoting myself to our Austrian guest, which I did most gladly. I arranged matters so that we were neighbors at the table for the conference meal. From the outset, the conversation developed in such a way that he was the speaker and I the one who listened and put questions.

The conversation turned quite naturally — even before we had finished our soup — to his studies in Weimar about Goethe and to Goethe's world conception. I became immediately aware that my neighbor possessed extensive knowledge in the field of the natural sciences. What was a great surprise to me was that he spoke of the crucial importance of recognizing the far-reaching significance of Goethe's knowledge of nature. In his scientific investigation, Goethe had succeeded in pressing forward from an external knowledge of the sense world to a deeper understanding which grasped its spiritual being. I had some knowledge of Goethe's natural scientific writings and of those portions in which he looks forward to an insight of which at present we can only have an intimation.

My table companion saw that he had an attentive listener at his side. He held the floor. We forgot that we were at dinner.

In the afternoon we stood about together, paying little heed to what was going on in the Theosophical meeting. When the conversation turned to Plato I was better able to keep up. But also here Steiner astonished me by drawing attention to hidden insights whose significance had not yet been rightly understood and appreciated. When Steiner asked me with what I was especially occupied in my theological studies, I answered that it was research about the historical Jesus.

Now I thought that the moment had come for me to take the conversation in hand and I began to hold forth about the status of the investigations into the historical aspects of Jesus' life, and about the question as to which of the gospels contained the oldest tradition. To my surprise I was forced to realize that a conversation on this subject did not develop. He permitted me to propound my theme without throwing in a single question. I had the impression that he yawned inwardly. Thereupon I climbed down from the high horse of my theological historical criticism and led it back into its stall, awaiting whatever might follow.

And then something remarkable occurred. One of us — I no longer remember which — came to speak of the spiritual decline of our culture as the fundamental, yet unheeded, problem of our time. With this we learned that we were both preoccupied with the same question. Neither had anticipated this of the other. A lively discussion then ensued. Each of us discovered from the other that we had set ourselves the same life task, to strive for the awakening of that true culture which would be enlivened and penetrated by the ideal of humanity, and to guide and hold men to the goal of becoming truly intelligent, thinking beings.

In the awareness of our community of interest, we took leave of one another. Destiny did not bring us a second meeting, but the consciousness of our common striving remained. Each of us followed the other's activity in later life.

It was not granted me to take part in the lofty flight of thought of Rudolf Steiner's spiritual science. I know, however, that he carried many with him in his thought and made new men out of them. Outstanding achievements in many fields have been accomplished by his pupils.

I have continued to follow the life and work of Rudolf Steiner with heartfelt participation: his achievements up to the first World War; the problems and needs brought about by the war; the courageous efforts to bring order into the confusion of the post-war years by means of the presentation of the ideas of the threefold nature of the social organism; the successful establishment of the Goetheanum in Dornach, where the world of his thought found its home; the pain which its destruction by fire brought him on the night of New Year's Eve 1922 to 1923; the courage with which he pursued its rebuilding, and, at last, the greatness of soul which he maintained in his untiring teaching and creative work during the suffering of the final months which he spent on earth.

He, for his part, also did not lose me from his sight. When my two publications, *Verfall und Wiederaufbau der Kultur (The Decay and the Restoration of Civilization)* and *Kultur und Ethik (Civilization and Ethics)*[10] appeared in 1923, he took notice of them and spoke in a lecture in favorable recognition of the presentation of the problem of civilization and culture which they offered, whereby he quite naturally made no secret of his regret that I sought the solution of the problem only by means of a deepening of ethical thought, without the help of spiritual science.

In my meeting with him, his countenance with his wonderful eyes made an unforgettable impression upon me.

Letter to Bruno Walter from Albert Schweitzer

Lambarene, Gabon
November 8, 1960

Dear Friend,

With one so overburdened and overworked as I am one must be tolerant. I am unable to accomplish, as I would wish, those tasks which are not part of the regular program. And, as a result, you have had to wait for the report of my meeting with Rudolf Steiner. I thank you for sending me the works which concern him. I have most of them in my library in Gunsbach, but it was simpler to receive them from you than to send for them from my library. To me the most valuable is the autobiography (*The Course of My Life*). Here one really learns to know him for the first time. What a pity that death took the pen from his hand.

I recount, as you will see, our meeting in Strasbourg, where Annie Besant introduced us to each other. Our talks are still very clearly present to me. They have had the result that I have occupied myself inwardly from that time forward with him and have always remained aware of his significance. What we have in common is that each wishes to see true culture replace unculture. We became aware in Strasbourg that we were united in common aims. He expected a renewal of culture from ethical thinking and from the knowledge won by spiritual science. In accordance with my nature, I had to remain with the thought that it would arise through steeping oneself in the true being of that which is ethical. Along this path I came to the ethical concept of Reverence for Life and the hope that an impulse for the renewal of culture may arise out of it. I know that Rudolf Steiner regretted my remaining in the old mode of thought. But we have both experienced the same sense of obligation: to guide men once again to a true culture. I have rejoiced about that which he was able to achieve through his great personality and his profound humanity. Each one must follow the path which is his own. ...

Write me, if you have the opportunity, a report of the commemoration celebration.

Cordially, your devoted friend, Albert Schweitzer

Letter to Bruno Walter from Albert Steffen

Most honored Herr Bruno Walter,

... Albert Schweitzer's recollections of his meeting with Rudolf
Steiner moved me deeply. I remember very well with what
appreciation Rudolf Steiner spoke about Schweitzer's *Ethics* as he
handed me an article for the weekly publication, *Das Goetheanum*,
with an almost imperceptible note of regret that this great friend of
humanity had not become a student, a knower of supersensible
worlds. What great significance an exchange of ideas between these
two thinkers might have had, especially in connection with the
problems of the people of color. Now, it seems to me, as if you, who
love them both, may yet bring them together.

Remaining constantly united in spirit and in gratitude,

Your, Albert Steffen
18 December, 1960

The Man, Rudolf Steiner

Andrei Belyi

*Andrei Belyi is the pen name for Boris Nikolayevitsch Bugayev, a very promi-
nent Russian poet, novelist and essayist. Born in Moscow in 1880, the son of a
well-known mathematician, he took his training at the University of Moscow
from 1899 until 1903, At the age of 22, Belyi published Symphony, achieving
fame in Moscow literary circles. He came to know Vladimir Soloviev, the
famous Russian philosopher, a number of whose followers later became
interested in Anthroposophy, and he immersed himself in the study of Soloviev's
lyrical and philosophical writings.[11]*

*He was also acquainted with Bulgakov and other well-known writers of this
period. From 1908 to 1912, Belyi wrote a number of books, establishing himself as one of Russia's leading Symbolists. In 1912, during a visit to Germany,
he met Rudolf Steiner in Cologne. From then on until 1916, Belyi stayed in
Steiner's vicinity, traveling along to hear him lecture all over Europe.*

*He became a personal pupil of Steiner's and worked on a novel, wrote a book
on Goethe and Steiner, and helped with the carvings of the first Goetheanum.
In 1914, he married the artist Assia Turgenieff in Bern, Switzerland. Belyi
returned alone to Russia in 1916. Active in various cultural endeavors and the
publication of several books, he also participated in activities of the 'Lomonosov
Branch' of the Anthroposophical Society in Moscow. In 1921, Belyi received
permission to leave the Soviet Union and came to Berlin, but his marriage to
Assia Turgenieff broke up at this time, and he reached a low point in his life
which even affected his relationship to Rudolf Steiner. But as related in the col-
lection below, a last conversation in 1923 with Steiner restored his attitude
toward his teacher.*

*Belyi returned to Russia, but increasingly the political climate there limited and
oppressed his literary activities. Only his early death in 1934 saved him from*

persecution and arrest. Owing to censorship and Belyi's opposition to Communism, his works were suppressed during the years of Communism. The sections below have been translated from his recollections of Rudolf Steiner that he wrote in 1928/29 and which were published in Germany.[12]

— *from an introduction by Maria St. Goar*
Volume 25, Journal for Anthroposophy

In the introduction to the excerpts from Andrei Belyi's book which appeared in the last issue of the Journal, the date of his marriage to Turgenieff was given as 1914, in Bern, Switzerland, as is stated in the German edition. (Perhaps this was a civil marriage required by Swiss law.) I have read, in Russian, many works which speak of him, and I also knew Assia — who lived in Dornach and died there — fairly well. The following is what I know and have found out about them.

Belyi was born and educated in Moscow. He came in contact with Theosophy in 1908 after his unhappy courtship of Liubov Mendeleev, the wife of his friend, Alexander Blok. He read Helena Blavatsky's Secret Doctrine and attended some of the Moscow meetings of the Theosophical Society. In St. Petersburg, he met Anna Minzlow, a then well-known theosophist and pupil of Rudolf Steiner. In 1909, he met the eighteen-year-old Assia Turgenieff (the grand niece of author Ivan Turgenieff) then home on vacation from her studies of etching in Brussels. Belyi spoke of his association with her as marking one of his seven-year life periods — from 1909 to 1916. She went back to her work in Brussels but returned to Moscow where they were married in 1912. They spent their honeymoon in Italy and a few weeks of that summer in Norway. Belyi wrote about those happy memories in his book whose title can only be translated as Notes of a Strange Man. On his way back to Oslo (then called Christiania), he saw Rudolf Steiner, whom he already knew of, and heard his cycle Man in the Light of Occultism, Theosophy, and Philosophy (GA 137). After this, Belyi and his wife followed Dr. Steiner on his journeys and heard most of his lectures from 1912 to 1915. He was called to the colors in that year and returned to Russia in 1916, while Assia remained in Dornach for the rest of her life. I heard Belyi read some excerpts of his latest works in the house of an aunt of mine. He read remarkably well about the building of the First Goetheanum and his stay in London on the way back to Russia.

This was my first contact with Anthroposophy, of which I then knew nothing. It is true that when he was in Berlin in 1922, Belyi became enraged with Dr. Steiner, who did nothing to obtain a visa from Switzerland for him. But his rage changed into adoration again when Dr. Steiner met him at one of his lectures and had a talk with him. Belyi lectured about Dr. Steiner and Anthroposophy on his return to Russia in 1924 and wrote his reminiscences, which could not be published in the U.S.S.R., where any spiritual movement was forbidden.

— From the introduction by Sonia Tomara Clark
Volume 26, Journal for Anthroposophy

Part One

Nothing of what I record here can convey a really true impression of Rudolf Steiner. More than once I have attempted to write down my recollections, but each time it has ended in a fiasco. The figure of Steiner in my story *Return* is an obvious failure. The attempt at a description in *The Beginning of the Century* was another failure. For my own use, I have tried sketching my connection with Steiner in his capacity as my spiritual teacher, and even there I failed. After this threefold shipwreck of my 'intention-filled attempts', I have decided on an informally sketched disorder of impressions of the Doctor (I ask the reader's indulgence to call him by the name we used for him then), and I shall indiscriminately collect together important and minor reminiscences. In order to grasp the expression of concrete life in Steiner, one must stretch one's own limitations. But I come up against a limitation in my own relationship to him, and so I can only describe him simultaneously with the annoying sense of my own limits.

One could say much about Steiner's work, about this mission of love and sacrifice, but it would sound commonplace because similar things are written about so many others. Steiner's sacrifice, however, surpassed anything that one can imagine.

I only want to mention his irresistible kindness. Its force did not express itself in gestures or spoken words. He never said, "I love, I feel," He made love visible indirectly, a faintly noticeable glowing sun-warmth around his mouth, around his eyes, that outlasted years and bore fruit in moments of despondency. He had, as it were, a therapeutic smile; his countenance blossomed in the abundance of perfect love into a barely discernible rose-exuding fragrance. He only 'bestowed' a smile, but one felt that one had nothing of the kind to give in return. He had the gift of 'the smile' — though he was never a charmer — and the faculty for direct expression from the heart. A giant of the power of kindness! His smile could have had a smothering effect had he not tempered it down when necessary. Many knew his sunny smile; we spoke of it. One must speak about it, for not a single photograph of his reflects it.

Alexander Michailovitsch Pozzo (1892-1941), a Russian lawyer, told me that when he came to a lecture cycle of Steiner's for the first time in 1910 in Bern, he had not the slightest intention of becoming a member of the Society. He thought he was sure of his way — another one — and traveled to Bern not to find anything but just to say farewell and to express his gratitude for what he had already received. But it turned out that this had been abstract thinking. "Until the next time," said the Doctor, and his face became, as Pozzo described it, a 'rose'. The above comparison originated with him.

Volumes could be written about his expressions of kindness of heart. The wisdom that retains in itself duty and love was great, but the force of love sometimes even surpassed the wisdom. The number of consultation hours increased, corresponding to the capacity for absorption; the time it took to hold six conversations was used to hold twelve. If one went to Steiner's (of course one had to have a previously made appointment), there was a long line of waiting people. When one left him, there was the same line, the car parked in front of the house, suitcases packed, but Steiner sat and listened, and how he listened!

Our last meeting went like this: a long line of persons ahead of me and behind me, the car was waiting. Steiner was scheduled to return to Dornach from Stuttgart. He greeted me and led me into the room. We sat down by a small desk. Steiner was pale as death; it isn't easy to listen to such large numbers of people one after the other when each one comes with his most urgent problem. His answers were always concrete and to the point, but they only unfolded their full nature in the course of the years. All this also passed before my mind during our last meeting. He turned his over-tired face with the good-natured eagle nose in my direction and said with a smile difficult to describe, "We do not have much time; try to say briefly everything you have on your mind." This conversation of twenty minutes lives within me as if it had lasted many hours, not because I would have been capable of saying *everything* but because he replied to everything beyond any words. The answer grew out of the facts of the following years of my life.

Only he was capable of replying like this, to recognize the leading thought of months and years behind the spoken words, and to discern behind this thought the sum of experiences, and to see my will that was not even clear to myself at that time. He thus replied to me *then* in regard to my thoughts of *today*. How clearly he must have 'seen' me! How concrete his relationship to me must have been. This relationship even surpassed the power of my love for him.

Of emotions — not a word; he had already demonstrated those to me before our conversation, during the conference in Stuttgart (1923), in the way he looked at me, stopping me in the hallway by holding on to my sleeve, pulling it a little, in the way he asked me to see him, entering the date and time into his notebook. In the smallest span of 'free' time between two lectures he was hopelessly overburdened with hundreds of consultations: and he shouldn't have been the one to address me but I him. He made his love particularly obvious by begging me to say everything that I had on my mind, and there was a lot on my mind, even many a harsh word against him. In his subdued, somewhat deep voice he explained to me in what respect and why I was wrong; and I felt how his atmosphere of warmth and fervor enveloped me too. Everything that I expressed was only three-dimensional, but this atmosphere of glowing warmth that purified me from my sins and my pain could not be grasped; this comprehension only developed in the course of years as the best in me.

A friend also described to me this warmth that seemed to emanate directly from the heart. She had arrived altogether unexpectedly, to leave again soon and for a long time. She had the absolutely urgent desire to be received by Steiner, but the Doctor was overburdened; he couldn't suppress the annoyed exclamation, "Why do you come during the conference? I don't have a free minute." And my friend replied in the same vein, "We cannot come whenever we want to, only when we are able to!" She turned around and walked away. She heard a voice calling her name and looked around. Doctor Steiner was running after her with outstretched arms; he took both her hands, was full of warmth.

Deeply moved, the late T. G. Trapesnikov told me of the force of the Doctor's inner compassion towards him. After a decision that Trapesnikov had made, the Doctor was emotionally so touched by the moral process that Trapesnikov had undergone that tears came into his eyes. At times when an emotional expression of his could not harm his students, his wisdom built no barrier between himself and them.

He wasn't in the least sentimental; instead he appeared rather distant and reserved, particularly when facing the temptation of sentimentality. And just because of this, Trapesnikov was so deeply shaken by Steiner's 'gift of tears'.

The Doctor promoted independence of spirit in his students and always awaited an opportune moment during which his help could become effective. Many a time I lamented, "My energies are failing; circumstances are against me." But the Doctor seemed to pay no attention. During get-togethers and lectures he gave no signs of noticing anything at all. Later on I realized that this gesture of ignoring me was an expression of his discernment: the soul seeking help had as yet not sufficiently matured in comprehension. One was required to persevere further since one's forces of patience had not yet been exhausted. His help was always an appeal to one's own consciousness.

However, in moments when life took on forms that were expressions of happenings within the soul, when the question of "to be or not to be" posed itself, then Steiner resolutely intervened in the course of providence with a courageous, energy-bestowing "Be!" And the collision culminated in catharsis.

Merely by counteracting temptation, and by his circumspect manner, he was able to direct his students to the beautiful and the noble without infringing upon their freedom.

In the fall of 1913, in Munich, I had to endure severe mental struggles. But he acted with particular indifference, even special sternness; there was reproach in his countenance. Later on I comprehended: he knew what he was doing; he wanted me to uncover the root of the evil within myself by my own efforts. One day during a concert, an image of myself arose before me; full of bitterness I was ready to give up. Suddenly in the first row, Steiner rose and looked right at me in such a way that this moment of self-recognition became enlightening.

He was a prompt and effective helper on the level of passing from one consciousness to another; he could wait a long time for a suitable moment. Maybe the everyday mind of 'Herr Doktor Steiner' was not always absolutely aware of the motives for his actions because he allowed himself to be carried by a spiritual rhythm not unlike the new teacher he describes in his mystery dramas.

He appeared in moments that required his presence, and more than once I experienced the strange fact that there were times when I did not encounter him though he appeared everywhere — on the construction site, during the lectures. Only I who lived across the street from him did not meet him. And then again he seemed to be in every conceivable place: Doctor Steiner here and Doctor Steiner there; one met him on the way to a lecture; I over-took him or he caught up with me; one met him during a stroll, on the way to Arlesheim where he did not go for weeks sometimes, with his umbrella and some package tucked under his arm; one ran into him on a street in Basel; suddenly there he stood all by himself in front of the display window of a bookstore. A strange rhythm according to which he could 'multiply himself' so as to turn up everywhere, be present everywhere. His own words came to my mind: "When an inspiration becomes active within us, our muscles pull us all on their own to the right spot where destiny awaits us."

In the spring of 1915, I believe it was in March, somebody tapped me on the shoulder quite emphatically when I was leaving the Schreinerei, the carpentry building, after a lecture. I turn around and Steiner stands directly behind me — very serious and very kind, almost fatherly. He winks at me and says: "Courage, Mr. Bugayev, have no fear!" But what was I supposed to be afraid of? I had doubts, I suffered, I wondered about some things — but fear? The reason became evident later. My states of acute fear lasted for months, a gloomy period during which I was nothing but one gesture — turned towards him imploring him for help. But he did not seem to hear me. These indescribable conditions of anxiety repeated themselves from April until August. And Steiner, who had foreseen them, had already equipped me for the battle in store for me with the demon of fear when he had come up to me and tapped me on the shoulder — "Courage."

Aside from his inner support, we also received external help to the extent that his physical resources permitted. When in 1914 – 15 people from everywhere congregated in Dornach and epidemics occurred (flu, called Influenza then), there was a demand for an anthroposophical doctor. We were treated by Dr. Fridkina, a Russian woman-doctor who did have a medical license but had as yet not practiced medicine. Fridkina had to report to Steiner about every patient. He was minutely informed about the course of each person's illness, gave attention to every detail of Dr. Fridkina's therapy, and advised her.

Steiner's elasticity, his ability to change within half an hour, was unbelievable. He possessed the gift of coordinating the expressions of many personalities, all living within him, into a unity, into an organization of personalities, a collegium. This collegium of personalities, out of which each individual one revealed itself freely and sincerely without limitations, was distinguished by a perfected individual style. The individuality of this style was none other than the higher self of the Doctor. In all of us, our ego reveals itself in the contradictions of our self-aware soul, in the collision of personalities within the context of the individuality encompassing them. In Steiner's individuality dwelled 'Manas';[13] and Manas distinguished his individuality from other individualities. It seemed to dwell in a different climatic zone above the storms, in the radiance and sun reflection of unencumbered snow-covered summits. The zone of the self-aware consciousness soul (in its usual form of appearing as the individual zone) is the zone of mists, of fogs. The zone of the intellectual soul is like the broadly sweeping landscape of Alpine pastures below, revealing itself to the observer as an abstract geographical chart; the zone of the sentient soul — it is the flowering world of green valleys at the foot of the mountain.

The 'Manas' of the Doctor — it is the snowy brilliance in front of the abyss of the firmament. But the Doctor moved about freely on all the soul levels below Manas, in the zone of the tempests as well as on the flowering meadows. From the dimension of storms he threw lightning bolts, he gathered flowers on the meadow; these zones were always alive in him. ...

The Doctor could be like a jester, capable of practicing like the "Joyous Science"[14] in front of his students when he thought it was appropriate. In such moments he appeared light-footed; by the way, he had a very light gait. If you saw him climbing the Dornach hill in the morning, you could believe that a slender youngster was approaching. Odd that this young fellow was wearing a morning-coat with flapping tails! Only then you noticed that it was the Doctor. Lightly and with agility he ventured up the hill and hurried from one wooden building to the next. Effortlessly he climbed the scaffolds, all the way up to the ones under the cupola, and there still higher onto the boxes in order to appear next to those working there and to explain his thoughts about a form. When he accompanied Mariya Yakovlevna,[15] he appeared to be floating along slowly by her side, arm in arm with her, but when he returned alone he hastened with light short steps down the hill; he seemed to be flying, overtook the slowly walking workers, turned the corner in a flash, and hurried with flying coattails through the front garden of the Villa Hansi. This is a sight that I have seen countless times because our little house was located directly opposite that of Steiner's.

From a conversation with Steiner, at the dinner table toward the end of supper: the Doctor is sitting on one side of the table, I sit next to him, on the other side sits A.A.T.,[16] and across from him — Mariya Yakovlevna and Fräulein Waller.[17] In front of the Doctor stands the almond milk that he is in the habit of drinking during meals; he looks at me sideways and remains silent in an expectant manner. I take this as an invitation to speak, and begin to talk about life in Russia. A.A.T. plays with a piece of paper. Steiner observes her for a good while, suddenly interrupts me, and points with his finger at the paper.

> Steiner: "If Mrs. T. persists in eating so little she will soon be thinner than this piece of paper."

> A.A.T., pointing at me and laughing: "If Mr. Bugayev continues to smoke so much he will be even thinner than I."

> I: "I have made a resolution to cut down my smoking."

> Steiner (looks at me from below with comical seriousness): "A smoker, who was in the habit of smoking ten cigars a day, promised his

doctor to smoke only nine from then on, to which the doctor replied, 'Oh no, by all means stay with your ten cigars; one more or less makes no difference!'"

Steiner had a style that ran contrary to any kind of moralizing. Sometimes he challenged me, and during teatime with him I was often in a mood for nonsense. He was completely different when he received a report on work: stern, aware of responsibility, intolerant of the smallest negligence. He demanded that people gather in silence some time before the beginning of his lectures. Here he addressed higher faculties; he spoke as higher self to higher self. To arrive at the lecture straight from the everyday rush meant the same to him as to arrive too late for communion, to push through the crowd in haste and rush up to the chalice.

When he noticed that in the Schreinerei in Dornach some of the members went in and out during the lecture, he asked that the door be kept closed during the lectures. He was punctual to the point of pedantry. He always appeared five minutes before the start of the lecture; he began to the minute. Tied to the schedule of meetings, courses, lectures, and class meetings in all the cities of Germany, he was constantly on the road, but everywhere he appeared at the correct time. During the whole period that I accompanied him, not once did he arrive too late or let anything be cancelled. "I shall come!" — and he came. It was said that he excluded some students from the *Hochschule* (the School for Spiritual Science founded by Rudolf Steiner in 1923/24 at the Goetheanum in Dornach) only because they had been late and in spite of that had come into the lecture room. He explained it so: either one wants to come or one doesn't want to come, but under no circumstances is one allowed to disturb the concentration of those present. He who does not understand this proves that for him the time to work esoterically has not yet come.

The way in which Steiner dealt with the problem of the sexes was markedly chaste. His formulation of the question was far removed from Freud's. Professor S. N. Bulgakov said to me once, "Steiner's ideology is sexless." That is not true. Steiner never closed his eyes to the significance of the sexes. He said, "The spiritual forces at work in sexuality ..." or "The spiritual forces inherent in sexuality ..." He merely emphasized that sex is not in itself these "forces," but is only the form in which they make their appearance. He stressed that it is dangerous to confuse the source of these forces and the form in which they are manifested. From this arise sexual aberrations.

He compared the forces of sex with the branches that stretch themselves heavenward, and their outward form with the roots of the tree. Indulging one's interest in sexual problems he considered idle curiosity that lays the roots bare. He never denied the roots themselves.

But he stressed that the ascetics as well as the followers of sexual philosophy have an exaggerated interest in the bared roots. The tree that is planted roots uppermost dies. The transformation of the powers of sex takes place through the intensification of the functions of that part of the tree that is above the earth, the foliage, which also provides nourishment for the roots.

The foliage is consciousness.

Steiner's seemingly abstract idealism is very concrete. He stood for the transformation of the spiritual forces within sex through the powers of the ego, for shifting the focal point of sexuality. The true evolution of sex is its transformation.

In daily life he was free and independent, and he welcomed all independence. It was whispered that he destroyed marriages. This criticism, like any distortion, was not altogether unfounded. The falsity of middle-class marriage that is no marriage at all, but an arrangement upon a sexual or economic basis, made him indignant. Ungenuine middle-class marriages burst at every seam when they came in contact with Anthroposophy. He did not take people who separated out of a love of freedom and drag them back by the ears into marriage. Every true marriage he greeted with enthusiasm.

An example of his independent attitude in matters of love: A married man complained that when his wife had asked Steiner whether she should return to her husband, she had been advised against it. Later the Doctor said to this man, "I know that you have been angry with me because I did not say to your wife, 'Go back to him'. But please think it over. Could I really have said that! You still love her, but your wife asked. If you love, you do not ask." Thereupon the husband, an admirer of the *Philosophy of Freedom*, understood him. His reproach against the Doctor changed into warmest gratitude.

In his kindness, the demands he made upon himself were unending. "Compassion has its limits," Mariya Yakovlevna said to him. But he replied: "No, compassion has no limits."

Of love he said: "It is a giving faculty. The more one gives, the more one has to give." Every true love, according to his words, has the quality of infinite extension.

He extended himself.

Part Two

The rooms in which Steiner lived all seemed similar to me; the similarity consisted in the extreme modesty of these always small, sometimes even narrow rooms. Nobody, of himself, could have had any idea that the Doctor lived in them. Whether he received me in an apartment given to him for his use by Countess Kalkreuth in her pink mansion in Adalbertstrasse in Munich, or in Bottmingen, a suburb of Basel, or in the apartment of the lady who led the group in Cologne, everywhere they were the same modest and small rooms He needed nothing more than a desk, a chair, books, a suitcase, a bed when he was a guest anywhere — that was all. At most, a curtain in front of the door.

Extreme simplicity, extreme unpretentiousness! His apartment in Berlin, where he spent many years, and where the doorman considered him a regular tenant, ... was reminiscent of a command post. For example, there in one of the small rooms was an eternally clattering Remington and the "ladies of the office." From this room emerged Fräulein Lehmann or Fräulein Hanna Mücke (a former Social Democrat), irreplaceable workers in the library and in the press, the Philosophisch-Anthroposophischer Verlag Both of these were situated in the same apartment building on different floors and were always full of visitors on private or on business affairs. Therefore the constant impression of breathless haste — out of the office, across the corridor, through the little hallway to the living room door, to the staircases, and there up the steps and down the steps from one apartment into the other.

All the floors of this apartment house were inhabited by anthroposophists. Here was the apartment of Selling, who had dedicated his whole being to the Berlin branch. ... Here, too, was the apartment of Kurt Walter, a fabulous, bright and always original human being, and his dear wife. ... Here dwelled the two Fräulein Lehmanns, who as children had been taken in by Steiner and Mariya Yakovlevna, (the Russian name for Marie von Sivers who was born in Russia and later became Marie Steiner). For years she was his secretary, confidante, and companion on all the lecture tours, master of ceremonies for all the meetings, custodian of transcripts, correspondence and typewriters.

And then there was the noble Dutch Lady Waller, temperamental to the point of extravagance: flying, short curls, a shield-bearer full of fire, always ready to draw the sword against surprise attack, or to meet one full of devotion. Sometimes, she, instead of Mariya Yakovlevna, accompanied Steiner; sometimes, during the rare occasions when Mariya Yakovlevna herself was away on a journey, she was Steiner's support — he who could be very absent-minded in everyday affairs. Once, instead of a book, he placed a houseshoe in the bookcase and felt bad about having to buy new slippers. Waller, opening the door to Steiner's apartment; Waller with a bouquet of roses; Waller in a white tunic dress and a stole of the same color; Waller, bending over the banister and talking loudly to someone on the floor below — behind her the Doctor's open living room door. All of these familiar, dear images so precious to one's memory.

All these inmates of the house, above and below Steiner's apartment, rushed in constant haste from one floor to another with papers and copies, clattered on typewriters and made telephone calls. My impression: Steiner's home is always open; its effect is like that of a cell in a commune where no one places any value on comfort; every minute is already scheduled; and there are tasks, tasks, tasks, tasks. Here, somebody is editing; there, admission tickets for a lecture are being distributed; here, books are being handed out. There correspondence is answered, and in between, something is corrected or somebody receives help. The whole many-leveled dwelling belongs to Steiner's apartment, and vice versa. In his house there are many mansions.

Rudolf Steiner and Marie Steiner-von Sivers, 1908.

And past these involved, restless rooms, and keeping the breathless ladies from their work, there stream, stream and stream all those who have announced themselves for a consultation with Steiner; all of them people who are really foreign to this bubbling life. But each one of them comes with a question that is more important to him than anything else in the world. Some of them come for the first time; they arrive as one comes to confession in the greatest state of excitement. And most of them are surprised. Instead of the dignified atmosphere they expected, they are received by loud, seething life that may offend their sense of propriety. They ring the doorbell with hearts aflutter — but the door is open; they are not received by the housemaid; in fact, there are no domestics at all. Instead, they are received by somebody who just happens to be there: Waller, Lehmann, sometimes even Mariya Yakovlevna herself. They are ushered into a small waiting room where every upholstered piece is occupied by waiting people. The room is tiny: a small table, a little cupboard, chairs, two doors behind coffee-brown drapes, very plain and anything but new. One door leads into the hallway, the other into the corridor. From here you enter a little corner room, and further on, a still smaller side room, measuring three steps square. In there is a large sofa where Mariya Yakovlevna used to chat with me in private; presumably this is the "salon."

The other door is here, directly in front of one's nose; a deep voice resounds behind it every so often. The visitor who comes for "confession" for the first time gives a sudden start. "What, the Doctor is here, right behind this wall?" One pictures the personal meeting with the "Teacher" within a certain ceremonial framework, but here simplicity rules and an atmosphere of intense everyday work where there is no room for ceremonials — hardly a fitting place for this teacher and the confessing pupil. In one of the back rooms there are probably some open, unpacked suitcases standing about. He returned yesterday from Switzerland and tomorrow he leaves for Hannover — and somebody is readying his luggage for a new journey.

Then suddenly, right in front of your nose, the door of this plain, "mystery-filled" room is opened, quick as lightning and with a total lack of mystery; and the Doctor appears — a little worn, with a tired, pale face; and, the perfect gentleman, ushers a lady out charmingly like a man of the world —

"Well, yes," — "It will be all right," — "*Auf Wiedersehen.*" His hand is raised in greeting from the threshold of the room, unless he accompanies her personally into the hallway, where he switches on the light, helps her into her coat, and closes the door behind her with his own hands. And then he quickly crosses the corridor leading past the waiting room, pushes his head through the drapes with a smiling, "One moment, please," and goes on into the dining room — perhaps in order to drink a cup of coffee. His visiting hours last for hours and hours. He gets no opportunity either to eat or drink.

The visitor is shocked; everything is more than plain, more than sober, more than modest. Particularly surprising is the Doctor's quick pace, the informality with which he thrusts his head into the room, his "worldly," polite-sounding manner. Sometimes he is in no mood for laughter. He paces hurriedly through the waiting room, even without looking up, with serious, stern, sad eyes, only to return immediately, "Who is next?" and to withdraw with the next person, sometimes for a very long period, sometimes for five minutes.

Occasionally the visitor is a foreigner and speaks not a word of German; then Steiner quickly fetches Mariya Yakovlevna. She is there right away; she who speaks many languages is his constant translator. He can make himself understood in French only with difficulty and with a pronounced accent. He was not gifted in languages. This side of him moved me. I was almost glad of it. It was extremely difficult for him to learn foreign languages, and I gained a certain feeling of security from this inability of his. It would be terrible to associate with a person who knows no difficulties.

He wears a tight, short jacket, a jacket that is no longer new. On occasions he wears slippers; his pince-nez dangle and dance on a little ribbon and sometimes become entangled in the drapes when he rushes through them.

And then you find yourself in his reception room: a tiny room, black furniture, books, table, an easy chair; everything very modest. ...When I enter here I immediately lose the ability to perceive anything except him, himself, how he sits down next to me, turning his ear in my direction (he hears less well with one ear).

And now the proximity of his profile disturbs me, the innumerable fine lines — not very deep, and drawn, as it were, by the needle of an engraver. I have never seen such a concentration, such mobility and such an involuntary play of lines. They gave rise to the impression that his face was constantly changing and that it would be impossible to retain this countenance in memory; but at a mere distance of fifteen steps, the lines were no longer visible and the face appeared smooth.

Sitting next to him — he holds his cheek, or rather his ear in my direction — one marvels at the lines. He does not appear to be fifty-five; rather he seems to be five hundred years old. The nose is particularly sharp and prominent; suddenly it is the nose of a griffin, but a benevolent "griffin." There are also lightning-quick transitions, or rather no transitions at all from the charming smile to the loud and clearly uttered pronouncement, in a deep chest-voice: "That is bad, that is very bad." Over such a "That is bad," often tempered again in the same breath, people could weep for many long nights, and their remorse last, not months, but years.

Simplicity remains simplicity, kindness remains kindness, but in the simple interior of this room there occur such dramas of every kind — dreadful and joyous ones — that … But it is of no avail to talk about it. He was, after all, "Rudolf Steiner," and he had the capacity to transform every situation into an unforgettable moment.

He was an enemy of any kind of pomp.

I was a visitor more than once in his reception room. I often had to come "for a cup of coffee" to Mariya Yakovlevna. There, one sat in the small dining room, furnished as simply as all the other rooms. One lifted the coffee cup to one's lips and knew: Steiner will come in directly from his desk or from the reception room. I recall how he once came out of the study, saw the coffee, Mariya Yakovlevna and myself, and immediately sat down with us. He slurped the coffee out of the little cup, convicted me of a frivolity, pulled out a few of my peacock feathers, all of this in passing, as it were, without completely interrupting his own thought, and he rose again without having finished the coffee. Evidently he was in a hurry to get back to his writing desk.

I remember: During a stormy and decisive meeting in Dornach, Steiner told the members of the Anthroposophical Society that the Society[18] would have to be dissolved if a way was not found to settle the conflicts that had arisen. This would mean that the extensive work on the construction of the Goetheanum would have to be halted; we would have to pack our bags and depart. The Goetheanum, surrounded by scaffolding, would be left abandoned in the autumnal rains. This was the gist of his address; he spoke as only he could speak, his words were like claps of thunder, his eyes were pitiless, searing flashes of lightning. In such moments his voice sounded like thunder in the literal sense of the word. I recall our depressed mood as we left the meeting.

On the following day the members of the Large Council and those attending the conference had to make a joint decision which it was hoped would put an end to the impasse of several weeks. This impasse was a continuing chain of conflicts within the Dornach Group, as the solving of one knot brought on a number of new ones, and these unending conflicts, were in my opinion, rooted in the suspicion against the Dornach Group and Steiner's co-workers. The "Tanten" (the "aunts")[19] spread rumors in various branch groups concerning the supposed goings-on in Dornach. From everywhere, self-appointed inspectors were dispatched to Dornach; the Large Council was called together. It came to a control action against the Central Executive (Unger, Marie Steiner, Michael Bauer) which was familiar with the internal political affairs of Dornach. The members of the Executive defended the members of the Dornach construction group, while the autocratic examiners tactlessly snooped around in the various spheres of Dornach. Marie Steiner resigned from the Executive, the investigations of the Large Council uncovered a number of conflicts that in the end all turned out to be gossip; bitter feuding erupted in Dornach. With every gesture, Steiner seemed to imply, "Leave my young co-workers in peace; don't you see where this will lead?" But the rumors, circulated for many months, supported the general prejudice against the "Dornachers," who were called the "Dornach hoodlums" in some branches.

Steiner's gesture was not heeded. The affair resulted not only in a rift between the old and the young but also in a split between the Branch Leaders, the Executive and the Dornach Group. Steiner wanted to call attention to this division within the leadership of the Anthroposophical Society.

Like a threatening cloud, he stood behind the rostrum and gave us a thundering admonition to take home.

On the following day A.A.T. and I were invited to supper at Dr. Steiner's after the meeting. During the meeting, a final decision was supposed to have been reached. The disentangling of feuds of several weeks' duration had worn upon all of us, particularly those working on the Goetheanum, to a point where some people suffered a genuine nervous breakdown. In the meantime, it turned out that the final settlement of the conflict no longer depended on those who had caused the confusion but upon those who were trying to untangle it. To the latter belonged those who had come from a distance in order to "revise" the life in Dornach, and now they themselves had to subject their consciousness to a thorough revision, leaving the Dornach working group to fare for itself.

During the meeting, it became obvious that a way out of the existing situation could not yet be envisioned. Steiner appeared for the meeting with a pale face in which something seemed to have been extinguished. He took his seat in the first row with the pronounced expression of an observer who has nothing further to say. His look seemed to imply, "Don't ask me anything more. I have warned you; you did not want to listen." From his posture, the manner in which he sat in his chair, one felt that he had "packed his bags," and was ready to leave everything behind.

His thundering was terrible, but still more terrible was the icy silence that surrounded him; in this attitude he reminded one of a glacier bounded by black and bottomless night.

No solution was found during this meeting, and a decision was postponed to the next day. Steiner came, sat, got up, and went out without uttering a word, with narrowed, tightly shut lips and a withering look of contempt, even disinterest! He left the meeting with an expression that seemed to say, "I can have nothing to do with it!"

We had the feeling that our invitation was an anachronism, that our appearing there would be like bursting into a house where a corpse is lying in state, this "deceased" being the Anthroposophical Society that Steiner had called into life.

We felt uneasy and let him and Mariya Yakovlevna walk ahead of us after the meeting, followed them very slowly and rang the doorbell. We stepped in hesitantly as one enters a house where mourners are gathering. But from the hallway we could see into the color-filled dining room. Around the table stood decorative red easy chairs, and in one of these red chairs sat Steiner, still in his overcoat, pulling off his boots (it was rather muddy outside). He was laughing with all his heart like a child. I shall never forget his eyes; in this moment they were the eyes of a child. On the table stood a bouquet of red roses, and I remember how he saw us standing in the hallway and waved to us with his hand from behind this bouquet in order to invite us into the dining room. And in this gesture of his hand there was a childlike exuberance. All evening long Steiner was in good spirits and joked and laughed heartily; sometimes he joked as if to encourage us to do the same. After the meal, during tea, he jumped up from the table several times, "Wait, I want to show you something," and disappeared to fetch whatever it was. I cannot recall everything anymore, but I do know that one time it was a volume of Goethe's works. In front of the red roses he read the wonderful poem by Goethe, *Roslein, Roslein.*

A.A.T. and Kiselyova, by the way, had presented this poem recently on the Dornach stage in a eurythmy performance, and even this had given rise to all kinds of rumors; the underlying text of the poem was supposed to be obscene. The reading and commentary by Steiner lent the poem a childlike, innocent tone; in his interpretation something slightly melancholy was added. One experienced a flowering meadow and a child that played with flowers, and above the meadow and the child a reflection of heavenly light.

The Doctor of this evening after the meeting lives in my recollections as a radiant, joyful person, almost like a child; perhaps I have never experienced him so cheerful as then. But the Doctor of the meeting remains in my memories as one who threatens, icily and without pity. Such icy contempt as on that evening I, anyway, had never before witnessed. The interval between the icy coldness and the cheerfulness was the time it took to walk from the Dornach hill down to the Villa Hansi, exactly five minutes. And in these five minutes Steiner's being had transformed itself. During the meeting he was one personality, in his home a totally different one. Both had revealed themselves in absolute independence of each other, sincerely and completely; the point at which they met lay, if one wants to put it that way, beyond the field of our gaze above the storm-zone — in the brilliance of snowy white summits, in Manas!

Steiner carried with him something stern and great, something so great that he appeared stern. He could not put down this greatness that he carried within himself — anywhere. Imagine something like this: Someone comes from a distant land with an immense, precious load. He comes to give it away, but it becomes evident that those who are to receive the priceless gift have no place ready where he can lay it down. The "place" for this gift has been cluttered up during years of drowsiness; the failure of the recipients foils the purpose of the gift. And this someone must remain standing with his precious burden although he almost breaks under its crushing weight. He must hold onto it though he thirsts to put it down for the sake of the others.

All this work, his stormy activities in the Theosophical Society and later in the Anthroposophical Society, served to prepare a fitting place which could receive the treasure. The final attempt to prepare a housing for it was the building of such a place; the Goetheanum was intended to be this dwelling. But the Goetheanum was burned down. This someone, who had come with the precious load, did not live to see the dedication of the second Goetheanum; he left as he had arrived, and took the most important part of the treasure away with him.[20] Though he gave so much, enriched so much, enough for decades, he could have given still more, for his treasure was destined for something far greater. This precious load that was carried by this someone often formed itself in my mind into the image of the Holy Grail.

All through his life, the Doctor carried the Grail before him. As he walked and even as he slept, he lifted up his tired arms supporting the Grail. This is the reason for the tone of sternness and the seal of suffering, an unbearable suffering caused by the impossibility of bringing to realization what he carried within himself. This sternness was, in a manner of speaking, the background of all the expressions of his soul. All these expressions had the effect of being out of keeping with the background of his life's mission. Everything peripheral stood out with particular sharpness and seemed so foreign that it gave me an inner shock; and the more he behaved in an outward manner, the more severely I felt shaken.

Rudolf Steiner felt that the battle with self-love was not a matter of destroying the roots of egotism, but rather of correcting its deformities. Egotism is rooted in the ego, in the spirit. The forces of the ego are submerged, compressed into the individual person. In a positive development, egotism becomes purified of its poison by virtue of the ego's discovery of itself in the place where formerly it had only found a "you" or a "he"; now the "you" could become the "I." The ascetic mortification of egotism by means of moral dogmas, mere dogmas, is equivalent to the maceration of sex through self-chastisement. The discovery of the point at which egotism is justified, Steiner saw as the goal of our wrestling bout with the realm of the personal. "Even though someone," he said, "may have started along the path to truth out of petty egotism, that is not so important. It is only important that when he enters the sphere of truth, he either leaves it or, if he decides to remain there, must relinquish his limited "personal life!"

This explains why, for a time, he not only tolerated pronounced egotists in his vicinity, but even turned his chief attention to them. He believed in the alchemy of self-knowledge; he knew that in some cases the path to truth leads through the visible emergence of a hidden vice. He had more understanding for sins born of activity than for those of laziness, indolence and prosperity. Occasionally weird, strange people turned up in the Anthroposophical Society, and he tolerated them as long as they did not inundate the Society. Of them, too, he expected the miracle of transformation.

He did not tolerate any self-satisfaction in merely following traditional virtues.

He was in the habit of saying, "It is better to think wrongly than not to think at all," by which he meant the ethics, not the logic involved. He considered thoughtlessness the worst of all sins. The thought that comes to a standstill is a habit; a habit that stagnates is an instinct; the firmly rooted instinct is death. Steiner wanted to liberate at least our thoughts in order to halt the death process in ourselves. All stagnation he considered retrogression and deterioration; and this deterioration begins with the feeling of self-satisfaction in traditional virtues.

In his opinion, some anthroposophists had "not been thinking" if they believed that through Anthroposophy everything would become clear and readily surveyable. He had stormed against such "exalted spirituality" in Dornach: "It just won't do — to have you running about constantly with such blissful faces and meditating, meditating, meditating! You could a least organize a group to further your education! Or simply sit down together and laugh a little and parody each other!"

Steiner's attentiveness was matched by sure keenness of insight, an ability to untangle complexities and give them distinct expression. For example: The story goes that one day the trains had gotten off schedule in a major railway station. (A through train was apparently coming in on an occupied track.) Aghast, the station master ran out onto the platform, unable to see any way of diverting the inevitable catastrophe. Suddenly, a cleanshaven gentleman appears beside him and speaks with him; not a minute passes before the stranger has grasped the situation; another minute and the station master, set in motion by the stranger's plan, quickly gives orders to the switchmen, the switches are thrown, and without incident the train thunders through the station. The stranger who averted the catastrophe was Steiner. His practical disposition demonstrated itself in an ability to orient himself in every realm — be it in the everyday realm of the railroad or in the sphere of ideologies.

Picture to yourselves, added to this kind of penetrating insight, the penetrating insight of spiritual clairvoyance. These two forms of insight, simultaneously active on different levels, altered Steiner's countenance strangely during decisive and important moments and permitted him to "throw the switch" for the intersecting movements of his soul with lightning speed: icy, ominous silence, then five minutes later a joke, and then the observation "Mrs. So-and-so is wearing this or that dress."

He paid attention to how a lady was dressed, and it pleased him if the gown were in good taste; I still remember how he walked up to Madame Péralté and gave her a compliment on her little hat.

He himself was always dressed simply, very simply; but everything that he wore looked good on him. The customary frock-coat in which he appeared for lectures and conferences was sometimes anything but brand new; still it produced an elegant impression; without making a point of it, Steiner knew how to wear it. To me, this frock-coat seemed part of his being, like the stubborn strand of hair that fell over his forehead and was thrown back again and again, either by the hand that held the pince-nez or with a movement of his head.

Everything he did had an unintentionally elegant and genial effect; and, along with his nose or his eyes, we all liked his soft, loosely tied scarf, a piece of black silk with billowing ends. I have also seen him dressed formally during a funeral in an old-fashioned top hat of peculiar shape, not too high and broadening towards the top. In this top hat, he looked like a figure in a painting of the forties, the forties of the last century, the years of idealism. They surrounded him with a breath of something ancient, almost old-fashioned which, combined with the brilliant marks of the new man, the human being of future centuries, made his whole appearance so impressive. In him, the present came to the fore least of all; it seemed to dissolve in the face of the future. It was the future that lived most strongly in him.

But he also had the gesture of the artist; a touch of the Bohemian — in the good old, but not in the modern coffeehouse sense. The free artist, the man of a free profession, made himself felt distinctly. I shall never forget a fleeting impression: Munich, a carriage rolls past me at a noticeable speed (the carriages are usually very slow in Munich). I am astonished by this fast-traveling carriage and even more surprised by its passenger, a smooth-shaven young man, on his face a daring, almost reckless expression. This was my first impression. He sits leaning back in a relaxed position, his cape fluttering, one leg crossed over the other, wagging the tip of his foot. This smooth-shaven young man supports himself by resting his elbow on his walking stick, and — so it seems to me — challenges the whole world to a duel from the height of his carriage. So it all struck me in that first moment, and in the second, half consciously: What is the matter? Where does he want to go? Whom does he want to challenge to a duel? And finally: My God! How could I be so mistaken? It is the Doctor! And I acted as though I hadn't seen him so that he would not see me.

I believe the reason for my embarrassment lay in the fact that in that moment, for the first time, I discerned in Steiner the "free artist," the "eternal student," perhaps even a "Viennese intellectual."

The impression of recklessness was naturally the wrong one. In fact it was really an impression of the fiery youthfulness that so often showed itself in him. The way he seemed — only seemed — to appear to me was the way he had occasionally appeared roughly twenty years before, in the circle of independent young people: among rebels, anarchists, revolutionary artists, and eternal students. Perhaps he had been like that in the group surrounding the anarchist Mackey, whom he was close to once. I hope that my reverence for Rudolf Steiner is beyond all doubt. But at that moment, I knew that it was with this expression that Viennese students, in the exuberance of untameable, youthful energy, demolished street lamps and played pranks on corner policemen, escaping unscathed.

But I have also seen Steiner during his "esoteric moments." Where is the brush of the painter that could catch this countenance? Where, in the Christ representations of Raphael, Rembrandt, Van Dyke, do I find what showed itself at such times on Steiner's countenance?

I also saw the Doctor in a soiled old smock when he plodded through the clay of Dornach in high boots. Then he appeared old, his face covered with innumerable little lines. In this humble, as if self-eclipsing get-up, he still looked wonderful. Handsome? No. One says that his was a handsome appearance. I cannot say. I never thought of it when I stood facing him. For me he simply looked wonderful — always.

He had, by the way, something pronouncedly Hungarian about him, something fiery, full of glow. His hair was jet-black; to some it seemed inappropriately black for his age, for there was not a single gray hair. And it was whispered that "he dyes his hair." Only in the year 1923, during our last meeting, without intending to, I observed gray shimmering through the raven blackness. "Poor man, even in this we haven't given you any peace. ..." The sight of these gray hairs filled my heart with sudden, strong emotion, impulsive love, joy, overflowing gratefulness that I had met this human being; and in my heart there resounded, "Thanks, thanks, thanks — thanks to you for every-, every-, every-, everything! And most of all for being what you are!"

Then came the farewell, and I am not ashamed to admit that I kissed his hand, because this involuntary, irrepressible gesture was the expression of a son's love.

He understood that: after all, it was he himself who, during the farewell in 1916, had embraced and kissed me just as impulsively and made the sign of the cross over me; that was the expression of a fatherly love.

Normally, he said "*Auf Wiedersehen!*" [meaning, until we see each other again] during a leave-taking. But this time he did not say that; after all, he could not lie. There was no chance of our meeting one another anymore. I never saw him again.

Like the huge boulders that are hurled thundering up into the heavens out of a crater, and then fall plummeting down from the heights, so there flies high up into the heavens the great tasks and ingenious projects that he posed: eurythmy, pedagogy, new religious consciousness, the idea of the abolition of the state,[21] the first and second Goetheanums. Many of his plans fell back upon him like volcanic rocks: the failure of his students in regard to his social ideas, the almost complete failure of the whole Anthroposophical Society, the burning of the Goetheanum, and so forth. These down-showering rocks deformed, destroyed the life of the volcano that hurled them aloft; but again and again he threw out new, magnificent ideas, high up into the heavens, until death set an end to his works.

I have never experienced anything more beautiful; for four long years I was able to observe this man in all his manifestations, in his greatness and simplicity, in serenity and storm, in love, wrath, and pain, just and unjust, laughing and joking. Has his picture, the picture of a simple man, grown dim for me? No! Out of all that I have understood and not understood of him, the main motif has arisen ever more clearly: enthusiasm, love, trust, and the joy that it has granted me by destiny to meet him. He is the real "unhoped-for joy" of my life, even in the "pain" that he unintentionally caused me; this suffered pain is a sorrow for the world, not for my temporal self.

After he had satisfied my old painful longing for the real human being, he brought me to conquer myself; he showed me the greatness of Man by humbling the "mannequin" in me; but this humbling took place for the heightening of truth.

My first meeting with him, in the year 1912, called up in me a jubilation of enthusiasm; today, in the year 1928, while I write down the sentences of these, my recollections, I can testify: with unclouded joy I think of Steiner — not a single shadow, not a single fleck of doubt!

Not many of my contemporaries have had the good fortune of being able to believe in "Man as such" as I believe — because I have seen the "Man" with my own eyes.

The highest form of all of Steiner's works was — the Man, Steiner.

A Postscript:

In her book, *Reminiscences of Rudolf Steiner*,[22] Assia Turgenieff, Belyi's wife, writes of her husband's departure from Rudolf Steiner:

Bugayev was deeply impressed by his parting from Rudolf Steiner, who said to him, "Many will find their way to Anthroposophy through you. Take care that when you lecture you never use the expression, 'so says Anthroposophy', but 'so I understand Anthroposophy' – for Anthroposophy is greater than anything that any one conception of it can convey."

"Was it hard?" Steiner asked as my sister and I returned from seeing Bugayev and Pozzo off at the station. "One doesn't know whether we'll find one another again," was my answer. "Yes, that one can't know," he repeated thoughtfully.

Part 3: Rudolf Steiner as Stage Director and Actor

The Doctor as stage director — that was an extraordinary phenomenon. You could write dozens of pages, describing his talent for improvisation: out of nothing, in five days, an actors' troupe; from a handful of rags, stage-settings; with a few musical laymen, creating an orchestra. And this homemade fare he would present to the anthroposophical audience gathered together from all over Switzerland in such a fashion that the guests from Geneva, Bern, Basel, Zurich and Lausanne cried out "*Ravissant!* Beautiful! Magnificent!"

He especially loved the Nativity play[23] which to this day has survived in remote corners of Germany; the text of this play dates back to the 13th century. He loved its shepherd jokes, the rough gestures that harmonize so well with the blunt, native peasant speech. He made it the custom for these "mysteries" to be seen in all the larger anthroposophical centers at Christmas time. In 1914, I saw them twice – first in Berlin, then in Leipzig. In Leipzig the people had worked on the production a long time before showing it to Steiner. In Berlin, Steiner directed everything with a light hand and in a matter of days the play was improvised.

I saw the Berlin performance on December 20, 1914, the one in Leipzig on the 28th or 29th of December; my God, what a difference between these two evenings!

The Christmas play in Leipzig: pompous, blown-up, ceremonial, conspicuously ostentatious costumes, theatrical in pose and expression.

Declamation, nothing but hollow declamation; in the huge hall, lit up bright as day, a procession, almost an act of worship, took place. But the whole thing was wrong, grandiloquent and boring; its worst aspect was the contradiction between the mystery trappings and the simple, powerful peasant speech. The stage director was the group leader, the author Wolfram, who prided herself on her good taste.

The Christmas play in Berlin: unaffected and cheerful, without any extravagant costumes. Selling, who played the devil, twisted two strands of his hair into horns, attached a tail made of paper to his Prince Albert coat — and already he was a genuine "devil," the devil of 13th-century folk plays. The Joseph was touching, and Fräulein Waller, unmistakably a "Fräulein," a Mademoiselle, with a homemade gold crown and a brilliant star atop a long staff, which she struck loudly on the floor as she made her way through the audience to the Christ-child, was an authentic Wise Man from the East, a king from head to toe.

After the Nativity play in Berlin, I walked home deeply moved, moved as after seeing a mystery play, thanks to the deliberate simplicity of the performance.

The Doctor sat in the first row and enjoyed himself; he laughed over the jokes of the shepherds and kings as if he wanted to add a dash of his own to the salt of the folk humor. And you could feel: his humor is folk humor.

After all, he himself came from the folk; he was the son of a minor railway employee. Again in 1915 and 1916, I was present at the rehearsals of the Christmas play. Now Steiner had more time to prepare the performance (in Berlin everything had been improvised within two days), and it turned into a real miracle. King Herod (Stuten) in some instances aroused absolute fear, and the devil bore not the least resemblance to the "little devil" portrayed by Selling. He was the devil incarnate, in keeping with this production, and outlined the Devil within the devil more sharply. In Dornach, it was the dramatic, in Berlin, the emotional, side of the text that was brought into prominence. At one point during a rehearsal, the Doctor bounded onto the stage, took the libretto and staff from an actor (depicting a shepherd) and himself played the shepherd who rejoices over the birth of Christ. He demonstrated how this shepherd sings and, supporting himself on his staff, springs round and round about it. You could hardly recognize the Doctor. His whole carriage was changed as in a rough voice he intoned the ancient, almost inimitable dialect. There I saw that there was in the Doctor a magnificent actor; had he not become the "Doctor," he would have become another Motschalov.[24]

On another occasion I witnessed how he took over the part of Mephisto in the scene where Faust dies and Mephisto fights with the angels for his soul.

"No, not like that, that's not a Mephisto!" he exclaimed. He sprang up onto the stage with one nimble leap, almost impatiently took the script from the startled actor, and began first to read the part of Mephisto with enthusiasm, then to play it, and finally confronted the eurythmist-angels as the very incarnation of Mephisto. A loathsome, hoary old man stood there on the stage. He was particularly repulsive and uncanny at the moment when Mephisto is bombarded with roses by the angels and becomes enamored of them. Right in front of the angels, the devil is transformed into an old man, a doddering old man who whispers dirty and pitiful declarations of love to the angels. This was not the Doctor anymore; this was the Devil.

At the conclusion of the monologue, he himself seemed surprised. He remained standing on the stage and wiped his forehead. "This is how one must act!" — Those were, I believe, his words.

That was great acting, no longer in a potential but in an altogether real sense. The following day I remarked to the Doctor, "Yesterday when you were the Devil, there were moments when I hated you."

He smiled a significant smile and replied with a sentence the exact wording of which I have not retained, but in effect he said: "We are 'occultists' in order to become acquainted with the manners and grimaces of that gentleman." (He meant the Devil.)

This conversation took place shortly before my final departure to Russia (1916). The image of evil as portrayed by Steiner equipped me with a knowledge that cannot be transmitted by any book. That play reached out far beyond the limits of the stage; you forgot that it was an improvisation. In this play, "play" was nullified. He was the Evil One himself. This is why I say that Steiner was a great actor.

The Doctor thundered just like Jaurès, in many different ways; really it was more extensive, but his silence during the pauses was even more manifold. Oh, the silence of the pauses! And the "stillness" of his appearance during the Esoteric Classes! It is probably the stillness of the Starets.[25]

Where is a model for his gestures and mimicry? Strange, the countenance was different, the eyes different, many movements different, the temperament totally different, but sometimes something in common emerged — in the flashing of his eyes, occasionally in the deep timbre of the bass voice, in the controlled, agile, lightning-quick movements (despite the completely different posture), in the elegance of the silhouette, in size — something in common with Chekhov, when, in the second scene of the first act of Hamlet, turning to the King, he says: "But no, my Lord, I have too much sun!"; when Hamlet addresses his father; when Hamlet appeals to his mother's conscience, or watches the approach of the procession bearing Ophelia's body; occasionally, the Doctor looked like that, not on the stage however, but in real life. I recall how, in the year 1914, during the General Meeting, he looked out from behind the door and searched for someone.

Picture the rich mimicry of Chekhov, encompass this wealth with your hand so as to transform part of the kinetic energy into potential energy, increase it tenfold and anchor it in a deep, absolute center — then you have a "model" and can surmise something of Steiner's attributes also.

Combine the sweep of Chekhov's gesture with the hand movements of Nikish,[26] if you can still recall him. Reduce Nikish's radius. Limit yourself to the small movements of the baton that guides the reins of a whole orchestra, instead of the baton give him a cross or the hammer of the Grand Master of a Masonic lodge, and you receive an impression of a "Master of a religious rite." I remember Bishop Trifon (Prince of Turkestan) during a religious service in the Cathedral of the Saviour, who moved me deeply with the supple energy, the beauty of the priestly movements with which his hand lifted up the cross; here too, starting out from contrasts, through a ricochet of the imagination, as it were, you can find something of the Doctor, the axis around which the gestures concentrate.

And if you dressed him in a Prince Albert coat and armed him with the dignified carriage of a strength that bears the weight of knowledge with superlative ease, something of the professor, in the best sense of the word, would be added. A similar elegant professorial demeanor distinguished Professor K.A. Timiryasev prior to his stroke, when in accordance with academic tradition, he appeared on ceremonial occasions with the three-cornered hat in his hand and the purple sash with medals over his shoulder. He knew how to wear this sash in a manner that evoked a reverberation of the red hue of the Marseillaise.

Strange paradox, an extraordinary ricochet! Timiryasev and Rudolf Steiner! Among dozens of facets, they had in common lightness, delicacy, elegance — and courage.

But among all those I have seen, with whom could I compare this countenance formed through and through as if with a chisel? I once beheld such a face; it was in the cathedral of Monreale: a praying prelate garbed in purple silk with a face that seemed carved out of stone like a cameo. But at the same time, you would have to see in this countenance the face of Erasmus of Rotterdam, though with a considerably smaller nose — also the face of the smoothly shaven dervish in Kairuan, the snake charmer. These faces, three axes in a system of coordinates, give rise in my memory to the basic structure of his face; sometimes it works. Ordinarily, it turns into a dozen fragmented portraits. Each contains only one trait — not, however, the countenance as a whole.

And with what could I compare his laugh, his open or subdued laughter? Such a laugh I have never experienced in anyone else. It was not the guffawing laughter of Vladimir Soloviev, though the same preference for roguishness was interwoven with earnestness and sometimes hid the most profound seriousness. However, the laughing Soloviev had a dreadful mouth; Steiner's mouth was one of disarming charm; it evoked the impression of a rose about to burst into bloom.

Sad eyes, small when seen close up — black; from a distance — dominating the whole face and like brilliant diamonds. The strand of hair falling over the forehead, the movement of the head with which it was tossed back – all this was reminiscent of a composer; and occasionally I recognized in the solemn attitude of his seemingly pure musical abandon to a subject the same expression that once in a Beethoven portrait drew my attention. Taken one by one, the features have nothing in common.

These shades that I beheld showed themselves in a still further nuance, the nuance of a fairy tale.

The friendly teller of fairy tales toned down the "sage," the "man of single intent," the "man of many sides," the "silent man," the "mimic," "professor," "Master," and so forth. The whole into which all these facets were gathered was that of a quiet and sadly gentle fairy tale.

No — I give up the attempt of producing a negative of his portrait by ricocheting aspects of other personalities back to him.

He had much of competence to say about the theater. This was confirmed by Chekhov's statement that his drama course gives an actor answers to specific questions of which neither the spectator nor the majority of drama critics has even an inkling.

The Doctor is, according to Chekhov, an expert, a veritable expert.

During each performance, new problems arose like mushrooms out of the ground. Speech, movement, costuming, lighting, everything which today is well-established in Dornach and Stuttgart — the Eurythmeum with a five-year training program and the Speech School in Dornach — was tackled and expedited by Steiner personally during the "mini-performances" in Dornach. This can be seen in the example of the breathtakingly daring attempt at a new scenic solution for the last act of *Faust*, consisting only of movement; the word was placed alongside of it and entrusted to a speaker; the speaker was Mariya Yakovlevna. The hierophants and angel groups were characterized through the colors of their costumes and veils. Special significance was accorded the pauses. For them, music was required.

Although there were, there in Dornach, representatives from all kinds of specialized fields, there were no professional musicians; but there was the composer, Stuten, and a few laymen. There was also a grand piano as well as a violin, a cello, a trumpet. Later on, two drums and a kettledrum were also obtained. For this group of instruments Stuten wrote music that was not bad at all and began to rehearse with the laymen. An orchestra came into being but it lacked a second drummer who was also supposed to work a "mystical" wooden rattle. I can't even remember today why I happened to volunteer as a drummer, probably out of the burning desire to help. Everything went well; under Steiner's guidance, I produced the thunder and the required shrill sounds of the kettledrum. The audience heard mystical sounds; the orchestral drum was meant to arouse a mystical tension in the spectators.

Taken by itself, each detail was paltry. The costumes consisted of rags and the members of the orchestra were, like myself, "second-rate drummers." But the total performance left a deep and strong impression, and in particular offered a solution for the staging of the "mystical" final scene of Faust. The first performance of this scene took place in August of 1915 at a critical point of time in Dornach life when our hill was enveloped in the sulfuric fumes of calumny and rumors arising everywhere from without and within the Society. The younger people lost courage. I believe that, among other things, the Doctor wanted to divert the younger people and confront them with a new task, but the effect of this *Faust* scene surpassed his own intention. A mystery quality flowed from the stage despite the inadequacy of ways and means. The breath of the Mysteries banished all darkness; the atmosphere became transformed. Up to the day of the performance, everything had been determined by hopelessness; then the battle between the good and evil forces began. We hoped for a victory and we won.

The turnabout of mood took place (through the effect of the Faust scene experienced as holy mystery) in the transformed atmosphere of Dornach.

It was a strange coincidence. A heavy thunderstorm came up at the beginning of the performance, and all the colors dulled. Outside, the windows thunder and lightning accompanied the words of the three hierophants and the ascension of Faust's immortal entity. But at the moment when the *Mater Gloriosa* made her appearance, the sun shone out through the dispersing clouds. We went to the performance on an oppressively humid afternoon under threatening thunderclouds; after the performance we stepped out into a shining, refreshed, sun-clear day. In this scene appear the words:

> *Lightning that struck flaming down*
> *To better all the atmosphere ...*

As I heard them, I thought: Yes, the atmosphere must be bettered — this air that surrounds us with its sulfuric fumes. During the performance, through the force of Goethe's words and the Doctor's stage-direction, a betterment of the atmosphere was achieved. This was in strange correspondence to the discharge of atmospheric electricity above Dornach.

The air was purified; the members who had been present went their way with bright faces, as after a holy rite, under a clear sky. In front of us, already at the foot of the hill, walked the Doctor. From this distance his black silhouette, against the background of the green, rain-soaked meadow, appeared especially graceful. Suddenly he stood still and with lifted arm pointed out the brilliant sky to Mariya Yakovlevna and Fräulein Waller. I imagined I could hear how he exclaimed: *The atmosphere is bettered now!*

It was then I felt that this gesture of the Doctor's, who cheerfully walked ahead of us (the day before he had been somber) and who, with outstretched arm showed everyone (not only Mariya Yakovlevna) the bettered atmosphere, is the gesture of a great master of the art of living, who works at one time through the cleansing word of a lecture and at another, through the purifying gesture of art.

This *Faust* scene, presented through the cosmic gesture of eurythmy, was for me in its effect something greater than art. It was white magic, theurgy, conjuration against the might of the dragon who, in Dornach, opened its jaws in our souls against the Doctor.

I knew: those jaws have been defeated.

Here I touch a point that can be put into words only with difficulty. In the tendency of the Doctor's stage direction, I see the attempt at communal play and clarity of style such that, under the veil of the play, something greater takes place.

I often had to think of the brilliant, ill-starred d'Alheim who had originated the *House of Song* and in his conceptions had something in common with Steiner. Like the Doctor, he contemplated the potentials of gesture in the last years of his life, a kind of eurythmy but, in contrast to Steiner, without being able to state anything decisive about it. In 1907-1908 when we were together frequently, he repeatedly said to me:

"The highest magic of art consists not in doing away with the agonizing contradictions of life through contradictory speculations, but to do so through rhythm, in a divine effortlessness akin to play." While suffering under the hardest blows of fate, in completely hopeless moments, d'Alheim would cheer us co-workers of the *House of Song* on with: "*Eh bien, jouons! Very well, let's play!*"

However, he himself did not know how to "play" and received many a blow when he wanted to do so.

Unintentionally — or perhaps consciously? — the Doctor promoted playacting during the difficult months of Dornach life when there seemed no way out. In the months of crumbling hopes, of dissension, of vilification and battles, during the months when many erred from the "soul-path," in the months when we, the Russians, could only remain in Dornach under the greatest of difficulties — Warsaw, Brest-Litovsk, and Ivangorod were then being evacuated — during this time of sinister encirclement, again and again the Doctor immersed himself in art for a few hours and achieved in those working with him the "divine effortlessness," the "playing" without which no one would have been able to cross over the yawning abyss of Dornach. There were several such "yawning abysses." I know that — and I know that often one single step determined one's whole moral existence. There were many among us who would have been hopelessly lost, had they glanced down into the depth below their feet. You could not go slowly there; you had to direct your glance up to the ray of myth playing above our heads and run; you had to be able to stride eurythmically.

There, before those whose glance was mesmerized by the abyss, stood the Doctor and showed them this light-footed striding; he himself ran ahead of us in "divine play," and we ran after him. He was Orpheus and made those dance who had become lifeless as stones. A.A.T., who at that time felt the least possible calling for eurythmy, glided across the stage, and I made the second drum resound.

The artist, the director Steiner, accompanied us across the abyss by not allowing us to recover our senses: performance after performance. During the productions, the mythos overwhelmed us; in the mythos the atmosphere was transformed, and the moment of transformation was a leap across the abysses. When we regained our senses – in February of 1916 – we already stood on the other side, the dangerous falling-off places lay behind us. Outward life in Dornach regulated itself; the front-lines were stabilized.

Then, the artist Steiner left us in order to do battle at other points for the tasks and members of the Society.

On occasion, the Doctor let the artist, the light-footed dancer, appear as the Orpheus mask of a new initiate, and the mystery of the new initiation flowed into the medium of art and succeeded where the brilliant, ill-starred d'Alheim had failed.

The motto of the Symbolists, Transformation of Life, stepped into view through the Orphic power inherent in Steiner, through creative symbols of the various "biographies" intersecting within him.

You might think that I want to represent Steiner as a "great" man. Not at all. The aspect of "greatness," the "greatness" of the Doctor, does not interest me in the least. I am not interested in quantity but quality; the color quality of his "portrait," apart from the size of the canvas on which the colors are applied.

The question of greatness is not appropriate in Steiner's case; I have seen many a "great person" in my life in whom I could not discover anything special.

The spark that falls into the powder barrel is tiny – the powder barrel is large. The Doctor is the tiny spark that causes great upheavals.

So-called "great men" are often nothing but a loud report that disperses itself in puffs of smoke, with no igniting sparks. Great fame is sound and smoke. And so the Doctor was not borne upward on the wings of his fame but has disappeared silently and unsung from the stage. He is the igniting spark that works soundlessly: its effect – ozone of the atmosphere!

Part Four: World War I and Building the First Goetheanum

The first task Steiner charged us with in Dornach, immediately after war broke out, was the care of the wounded. He mobilized everybody who knew anything about it and asked that we take a course in first aid. At that time there was no way of predicting which direction the actions would take. We were situated directly at the border. For a week everybody expected the war to extend to Switzerland as well. The German cannons in Baden were already turned our way, since the French army unit stationed close to the border might penetrate Swiss territory during its retreat to Belfort, a French fortification, and thus violate Swiss neutrality. The units would march through our valley and Baden would open fire on Arlesheim and Dornach. This was obvious to the Doctor from the beginning, and he induced us to learn how to bandage and transport casualties.

A mood of panic predominated; people ran screaming out of their houses into the street. The nearby thunder of the cannons would not cease; it was rumored that the border had already been crossed and that there was street fighting in Basel. General mobilization began in Switzerland; the federal trains and streetcars were to be employed for military purposes as soon as fighting should break out on Swiss soil. The civilian population was to evacuate into the mountains after the alarm was sounded; the defense of Switzerland was to start at a point above Dornach; directly above the Goetheanum artillery was positioned. Our whole area was turned over to the war.

People packed, vehicles were made ready in preparation for flight into the mountains. One day we were called into the canteen, asked to have money and luggage within hands reach, and to sleep fully clothed at night. The alarm was expected during the night. We were to gather in front of the canteen and then proceed into the mountains together with the Doctor.

He was taciturn, calm and sad. We usually saw him in the canteen where we met at lunchtime, for afternoon tea, and in the evenings. At other times he had rarely been there, but now he came daily, walked about among us, or sat down somewhere on a bench. He looked infinitely tired. He came for no obvious reason; he only wished to give us courage with his presence.

But it became clear: life in Dornach, the Goetheanum, we all were in danger.

I remember a meeting with him; it was during the hours when we heard the first boom of cannons. We knew – there was war, but we had the feeling: it is far, far away; Switzerland is a neutral country and we have a roof over our heads.

But suddenly one evening after work, A.A. T. and I went down the hill to Arlesheim; in front of us the peaceful little houses of Dornach, beyond it in the distance, the flat country. There, on rare days, one can see the mountain ridges of Alsace, though usually the plain dissolves in haze. But what is that? Thunder? An odd, short rumble. The line of haze is different; is that rain? Is that fog? Or smoke? Probably a thunderstorm coming up — and below, between Dornach and the hill, stands a lone black figure. Someone has stopped on the street with bent head, irresolute, as if listening. What is he waiting for? The thunder perhaps? We look at each other: Why, that is the Doctor! But why is he like this — without his accustomed certainty? Why does he hesitate and seem not to know whether to go on or not? He remains standing and listens to the thunder. Is this indeed actually thunder? We are in Switzerland, in a peaceful country; it cannot be otherwise; I don't even want to think the thought that begins to form.

The Doctor, who has seen us, waits for us. Without greeting, he points with his eyes into the rumbling distance, and I hear his deep voice: "The roar of cannons?" There can be no doubt — that is artillery. There was fighting around Basel about this time and a French army unit was being pushed off towards the Swiss border. It was the thunder of cannons. The three of us stood there in silence; then we wanted to go on. He barely acknowledged our farewells and went on with lowered head, undecided, his ear still turned in the direction of the dull rumble.

In Arlesheim people already knew: that is no thunderstorm; those are cannons; the layer of haze over the plain is smoke. The next day it was in the newspapers: "The battle near Basel."

The first reaction to the war: we must commit ourselves more emphatically to our common cause; all of us — Russians, Germans, Austrians, French, Poles — we are all brothers in misfortune, we are all victims of criminal politics; our "politics" was devotion to the common cause, determination to continue building. When Strauss, the Bavarian, was drafted and had to join the services as a medical aide, he noted down as many Russian words as possible so he would be able to help wounded Russian prisoners. The motto that united us was "Love, Solidarity, Responsibility." We experienced our solidarity even more vividly during the days when panic broke out everywhere. The anticipation of an exodus, together with the Doctor, resembled something Biblical.

But gradually calm returned; Swiss troops from all branches of the army were stationed in our vicinity, and when the border had been sealed with a mine barrier, the feeling of danger subsided. We continued carving on our building, aware of the fact that it could be destroyed at any moment by artillery shells. Added to this were new worries: hordes of soldiers, some among them intoxicated, passed through the area. Occasionally they advanced as far as the construction fence where they laughed and smoked between the huge piles of wood shavings. This was extremely dangerous; the whole hill could easily have gone up in flames — five wooden barracks, the office, the Goetheanum itself, and mountains of wood shavings. The men took turns standing guard day and night. Some days, particularly on Sundays, whole groups of artillery soldiers came down from the Gempen[27] and congregated in front of the Goetheanum: "What is the matter?" "We want to take a look at it!"

One Sunday we were in the canteen; the Doctor was there too. People gathered around him with newspapers in hand and the newest state of affairs was discussed. He put on his pince-nez and listened. I don't remember anymore why I had to go up to the construction site. The road ran up between the canteen and the Goetheanum to the Gempen; there, the footpath ended which led from the hill past the barracks and the Schreinerei (the carpentry building) to the gate of the construction fence.

In front of this gate I saw a group of soldiers, thirty or forty men, who absolutely wanted to see the construction site. Our guards — von Heydebrand and someone else — wouldn't let them in: "No entry to unauthorized persons!" More and more soldiers were joining the group. Already annoyed, they demanded to be let in. I reflected that this could have unpleasant consequences; either they will gain entrance forcefully and set fire to the Goetheanum with their seventy burning cigarettes, or our relationship with them will be hopelessly ruined, something that would entail no end of difficulties. Our guards did not possess particular presence of mind; soldiers must be received differently. I elbowed my way through to the front, pushed the guards aside and addressed the soldiers: "Come in, friends! We'll have a guided tour for you directly! Wait just a moment."

I saw the indignant faces of the guards; I saw additional groups of soldiers coming from the Gempen, and I ran along the street to the canteen as quickly as I could, calling already from a distance: "Herr

Doktor, Herr Doktor!" The Doctor, who had understood right away that something extraordinary had occurred, came towards me with agile, quick steps, almost running: "What's happened?" It all fell into place. Hurriedly, while we were walking up together, I explained what had occurred, urging that the soldiers be let in — it concerned the building after all; even the Doctor himself was not the main consideration here. He grasped the whole situation immediately. We rushed up together; in no time he stood in the midst of the soldiers, smiling, friendly, impartial, and said that he would guide them personally. We all entered the construction area together. All cigarettes were extinguished.

Steiner led the soldiers around the site for a good half-hour. In conclusion, he climbed up a scaffold in order to show them the forms and to demonstrate our manner of working. "I'll show you; go fetch a chisel and hammer!" Someone ran off and returned with both. The Doctor himself began to carve so that they could see the process right on the spot. The soldiers watched with shining eyes.

We returned friends: the Doctor, the guards, I, and about a hundred soldiers; their faces were open and cheerful. They obviously had difficulty in finding the right words to express their delight at the courtesy with which Steiner had guided them and seen them off. From then on, the very best relationship existed between us and the army units stationed nearby. We had set visiting hours. I, too, had to take on such guided tours.

The outbreak of the war had brought Steiner new, special problems; he had to guide the outbreaks of nationalistic sentiment into sensible directions. Three weeks later the first momentum of our spontaneous solidarity was quite evidently broken. All through September and through all of October the storms in the canteen did not abate: the British and the Russians gathered together in little groups, the Germans often insisted very tactlessly that the war had been instigated by the provocative attitude of England; the Russians countered with the statement that a breach of neutrality amounts to barbarism. Soon, theoretical debates changed to concrete incidents and endangered the whole life of Dornach. Schuré's withdrawal from the Anthroposophical Society, the nasty rumors that filtered out of France via the French part of Switzerland, the duplicity of some Poles — all this had very negative effects. All eyes were on the Doctor; one secretly hoped that he would at last state: "Germany is in the right!" or "Germany is to blame for all the catastrophes!" However he did not accuse a single country, only the mendacity of the press, and he recommended that one not believe the sensational news reports and instead work undauntedly on the human aspect of true culture. ... Everybody waited tensely for an unequivocal gesture.

One such gesture lay for me in his five lectures concerning the essence of culture which he held in our Schreinerei in November. They contained living representations from Italian, French, English, and German culture: Campanella, the 17th century in France, the German "Frenchman" in Steiner's depiction, Leibnitz, Shakespeare, Newton, Schiller, and Goethe. An image of Russia arose — the Russia that is striving towards the future, the kingdom of the spirit. Everybody was enthused: the French, the Austrians, Germans and Russians. The Doctor had succeeded in smoothing the waves of nationalistic passion by pointing out the unity that all great culture has in common. In the light of his words we once again turned to one another; the oppressive atmosphere was transformed. Later on other infections appeared, but the nationalistic fever was once and for all overcome; from then on, the members of the various nations at war with one another lived in peace.

The year 1915 — a sea of problems that spilled over into the continuing daily life of war. This even made itself felt in Switzerland and was intensified by our particular location. In regard to mastering the artistic tasks, the difficulties of communication mounted due to the dogmatic attitude of artists oriented towards academic, impressionistic or futuristic directions. In working out the tasks posed by Steiner one had to come out in one's true colors; in the glass-house[28] two factions formed. For example: in the "childish" designs for the glass windows, one side saw the expression of new and original direction in style. The object — symbols of the path of initiation — aside from its aesthetic value was evidence that the author of these sketches was a spiritual leader; consequently, in executing the details of these sketches, spiritual realism had to be maintained. This was the opinion of Thaddaeus Rychter, to whom Steiner had entrusted the glass windows even before the laying of the foundation stone and who led the work in the glass-house until the fall of 1915. This was the opinion of Assia Turgenieff, that of Ledeboers, and of the Berlin painter Fräulein von Orth, who later married the Russian K. Ligskiy. It was the opinion of Ligskiy, with whom nobody could compare in endurance and wealth of artistic ideas.

But Rychter was drafted and had to leave Dornach. The glass-house was placed under the leadership of Siedlecki, whom Rychter had called from Poland and who had a high opinion of himself. According to his thinking, Steiner's sketches were naive and helpless; he executed them in the direction of an outwardly most effective but hollow modernism ala Wyspianski[29] and prevailed in this against his fellow workers. They believed that the Doctor's idea had to be preserved at all costs, that some of the valuable panes had been ruined because only cheap modernism and nothing of Steiner's original conception could be discovered in them. The younger ones tried to save the style of the original designs as much as possible and terrible scenes took place in the workshop. I, too, gnashed my teeth together in anger many a time when I found myself confronting the plain stupidity of the "genius" from Warsaw.

Rumors of tensions in the glass-house mobilized the authorities in the construction office. One day, Dr. Grosheintz appeared to inspect the workshop — but what did he, who had only Boecklins hanging in the office of his dental practice, know about it? Siedlecki prepared a pompous reception for him and had a way of duping him immediately with modernistic truisms. We tore our hair in desperation when we heard that Siedlecki's style had thus been officially accepted. This meant that Steiner's style was rejected just as officially. The new technique of glass grinding, used here for the first time, the material itself, the tremendous achievement of all the workers — it was all very impressive, but not Siedlecki.

And the Doctor himself? How did the Doctor react to all this?

When he contemplated the details of the work done in carving, engineering or in working with concrete — and he involved himself everywhere energetically — he only acceded to the wish of those at work. For example, when the carvers expressed the desire to penetrate his designs to the innermost fiber, he came daily and stopped at each group in order to trace certain sections with charcoal. He was convinced that he was expected here and that his suggestion could in fact make the work easier. For the sake of this direct contact, the carvers had refused the leadership of Kacer — who had been placed there by Steiner himself — when they noticed that she did not do justice to Steiner's intentions. Kacer's duties were jointly taken over by representatives of all the groups; there were the various groups and Steiner was the coordinator. The work progressed beautifully. This "anarchy" saved the idea of the whole; the "monarchy" would almost have destroyed it.

The same thing could have taken place in the glass-house; the glass grinders were dreaming of it. Rychter was not the "boss"; he was a comrade; the Doctor visited him daily. But suddenly a "monarch," a genius, appeared in the "Rychter-house," as we called the glass-grinding workshop. He introduced such an atmosphere there that the fellow workers could only gnash their teeth, and the Doctor quietly withdrew. Prior to his departure, Rychter, who had brought Siedlecki from Warsaw himself, and now regretted his mistake, tried to move heaven and hell in order to exclude Siedlecki as "heir apparent." He suggested that A. A. Turgenieff take over the workshop for the sake of form, in order to save the autonomy of the group of glass grinders, but A. A. Turgenieff shied away from this responsibility and from intrigues of the star from Warsaw; the suggestion was not realized.

The Doctor, who tried hard to avoid any intrigue which might cause additional complications due to the war situation, knew very well that this "Pan" had already made critical note of Steiner's sympathies for us, and that being a convinced "entente-ist" of Catholic character, Siedlecki could well become a dangerous political factor in Dornach. His sharp tongue could have caused much trouble, and enough rumors wrapped us round as it was. The Doctor "gave up" on the windows in favor of the effort as a whole. He stayed away since he was not asked; occasionally he passed by just to keep up appearances, conversed noncommittally and praised the masterly execution. Siedlecki's work had a superficial polish, a certain cunning, the flourish of a gifted nature. And the Doctor was concerned that this "character" that rejected him should not simply abandon the work at a critical moment.

When the conflict with the younger people who sided with the Doctor came to a head even in the glass-house, he withdrew. The fate of the glass windows was decided by a dentist whose taste did not rise above the sweetish flavor of Boecklin. The Doctor left the field of "politics" to others; in his direct way he concerned himself with what was nearest at hand.

Doctor Grosheintz, a well-to-do dentist with Boecklins hanging in his waiting rooms, and young people, futurists and superfuturists, among them some older rebels with young hearts, for instance old Wegelin — this mixed group summoned up all its energies with ardent zeal to steer the Goetheanum safely past various points of danger. This caused collisions between the younger members and the dignified members rich in years but poor in artistic experience. Frequently, tensions were brought to a head in the proscenium, the cause of which lay far behind in the wings.

Dr. Grosheintz did not have much good to say about Germans at that time; the militant "Germans" among us gradually stirred up the "highly explosive" young people against Dr. Grosheintz. The pretense was that the house which Dr. Grosheintz wanted to construct from an already-existing model by Steiner would be too close to the Goetheanum and would obstruct the view towards it. Actually, they simply wanted to drive Dr. Grosheintz off the hill. The spark ignited; the explosion was not long in coming. We raised the alarm: "What! Citizen Grosheintz wants to locate his middle class, one-family dwelling in front of our Goetheanum? We won't tolerate that! We shall tear our hill from the hands of its owner!" The older ones fueled the fire and called a meeting of the woodcarvers under the chairmanship of Wegelin. A resolution was composed: "We, the artists and woodcarvers, demand that no private buildings be erected around the Goetheanum! We cannot allow laundry drying on the wash line around the temple of culture!"

Dr. Grosheintz was disconcerted; he wrapped himself in silence; the construction office sympathized with us.

When Doctor Steiner returned from his trip and heard about this affair, he became very angry. With great emphasis he made it clear to us that our resolution consisted of prejudices. The style of Grosheintz's house did not hurt the general style; a wash line was by no means a desecration of the Goetheanum. Such a claim could only arise from a lack of understanding for the mission of the Goetheanum, which strives for the reality of the new life in all its facets and tries to unite the temple and life. A conception that would eliminate the temple from the concerns of the ordinary day and ordinary human life would be nothing but sentimentality. The new anthroposophic life includes wash lines around its building. I believe he said on that occasion: "Here particularly, diapers should flap on the wash line in the wind."

He did not care about "politics" of this kind. Regardless of all the differences in social intricacies, the younger generation and people such as Dr. Grosheintz served the common cause with great unselfishness. Dr. Grosheintz made his contribution; he sacrificed his property. The young people made theirs — they sacrificed their time, their energies and their health. The intrigue of the "politicians" had failed.

Without curtailing our freedom, Rudolf Steiner familiarized himself thoroughly with the concrete, given facts of the various work areas. His participation extended only to the outer execution, the technical components of the task. We could follow our own intentions freely in the interpretation of his plaster models; their dimensions were infinitesimally small in comparison to the wood blocks. Neither the edges nor the number of planes could be discerned from the model. Each form could be interpreted in various ways as an interplay of five, four or nine surfaces. The leader of a group had to feel out the surfaces — the potential — of the form. He had to explain this to his fellow workers, calculate it, mark it on the wooden block and carve it out. The Doctor did not intervene in this process. He inspected the architrave when its forms were already discernable, and, together with the carvers, engrossed himself in the interplay of the intersecting surfaces. Again and again he advised starting from the plane rather than from the edge or ridge; the ridge comes into being of itself as soon as the planes intersect one another. In his lectures he gave us a detailed reason for this method. In the end, when the form was already emerging, one was faced with the task of either reducing or increasing the number of planes. There, too, one could count on his advice. One could trust his sharp eye — the sharpness of his eye was unerring.

The form appeared unaffected and fresh when carved "out of the plane." It seemed to shed itself out of the wood block of itself. One avoided geometrical rigidity. The effect of carving from "edge to edge" unfailingly appeared feeble and static. When one carved with the gouge from a pre-marked edge, humps and holes formed that required repeated corrections and new carving. In making such corrections, one often reduced too much of the form, yet each point of the huge whole could not be lower than a set number of centimeters below the surface that was at a right angle below the highest point. All points had to harmonize in their proportions. If one took off two centimeters at one point, one had to take off forty at another, ten at a third, at still another three, and somewhere else sixty centimeters. Too much at one point was too much everywhere. The huge forms were supposed to blend smoothly into each other. This seamless joining had to correspond with the static function; we always had to keep this smooth blending in mind. In case of doubt we were required preferably to leave a little too much rather than to shave off too much because something that was left could easily be corrected afterwards without any difficulty. If one took off too much, important sections were missing later on which had to be put back on. This was not always possible and very expensive besides. During the war, no oak could be imported from America for the exterior facing, and the wood already on hand was becoming depleted.

In a word, we guarded against taking off too much as one guards against fire. Practical experiences, not just aesthetic considerations, proved the Doctor's directions to be correct: that is, to work out of the plane without thinking about the edge.

A completely unexpected rhythm thus revealed itself in such a form. In the method of treating the planes, the same law came to expression which the Doctor represented in everything: the edges that determine the contours of the form are like the accentuation in a verse or the note in a melody; the surface that comes into being between the edges of neighboring facets corresponds to the poetic pause or the interval. Later on, Steiner pointed with emphasis to the significance of the pause in the rhythm of speech and to the importance of the interval. At this time he stressed the significance of the plane, the "pause" between the edges.

The birth of form out of rhythm — this is what he proclaimed to us.

Again and again he said: "We are trying to develop a total style in building, which originates neither from some abstract purpose nor from a — perhaps very profound — allegorical consideration. Instead, we stew this style in the juices of its own depth, as it were, where the intellect is silent and the creative lives."

Another time he said: "We bake our building — please forgive this expression — like a cake." With this he wanted to say: the whole thing rises like dough. It realizes itself in the interplay of various ingredients; the result of this interplay, the total style, is a surprise.

In realizing the intentions of the construction, it was this moment of surprise that concerned him. In this he was like Nikish, who explained the musicians' tasks to them in great detail during the concert rehearsals in order to make the style — the result of the confrontation between the community of musicians and the symphony — audible in the concert and to make it artistically complete.

In like manner the Doctor conducted the formation of the whole building. All areas of work — carving, glass-grinding, painting, construction of the cupola, the pedestals, the row of columns — all were instruments for him, and he tried to make the symphony resound in the interplay of the orchestra. It was clear to me: some musicians understood what his intentions were; others (Siedlecki among others) did not care about the sound of the orchestra but about the tremolo of the violin solo at the expense of the Goetheanum.

Until my departure from Dornach, I worked on the ceiling above the main portal. I stood on a scaffold; directly in front of my feet Ligskiy carved on the window from outside; sometimes he poked his head inside; sometimes I poked mine out, and we talked with each other. When I thrust my head through the opening, I saw the concrete terrace below, the hill, Dornach, and the distant view. The Doctor was still not back — he was on a lengthy journey — and the thought that I would have to leave Dornach for a long time without having seen him once more worried me.

One beautiful clear day, the shout went up on all sides: "The Doctor is back!" My heart missed a beat. I would see him once more after all. About five in the afternoon I hear a voice, "The Doctor!" Covered with grime and dust, chisel in one hand, hammer in the other, I squeeze on all fours through the opening and see the Doctor below, radiant, joyous, in his morning-coat with the black, wide-rimmed hat. By his side Mariya Yakovlevna in rose-color with her shining golden hair. I, still on all fours, chisel and hammer in my hand, wave to them from above; he raises his hand high over his head, a charming smile and a resonant "*Gruess Gott!*" In his spontaneity and in mine, there was straightforward affection. This is how close relatives, children and parents, greet each other.

This is how we met when he came to see us.

Part Five: Rudolf Steiner and the Theme of the Christ

When the Doctor spoke to us "head to head," we could take it in. But at other times he addressed himself to our hearts. "From heart to heart" — what a clear, loving smile accompanied his words when he spoke about the Jesus child lying in the manger in all the power of His helplessness, the manger against which Ahriman's sword was shattered! Then the Doctor himself had something of a helpless child about him and asked naught for his own speculations. He was all heart: or better, his intelligence had moved into his heart, and the intelligent heart blossomed forth; the "heart" — not an "intelligence with heart."

I want to repeat so as to make it unmistakably clear: The Doctor had brilliant things to say about Gnosis and the Christ; that is well-known. But anyone who has not himself experienced Steiner cannot really form any idea of what took place in our hearts: "He was more heart than head." He was inspiration, not only imagination. His words about the Christ were inspirations — heart-thoughts that transformed hearts more than the heads. ...

When the Doctor spoke about the Christ, his head was silent; he spoke out of the sun-filled heart. The words of his lecture cycles on the Christ are like an exhalation — not of oxygen, but of carbon dioxide, the symbol of mysterious life processes. ...

The Doctor stood "close to the door," but not to this door, the wooden door toward which the heads turned. One ran one's head against the wood — and lost consciousness. But there was another door — the heart — and it was to that door he called us. ...

You might think, "Nonsense! What doors is he talking about?"

I speak of those doors through which you shall not enter as long as you have not changed your whole world. One must speak of it differently, without the acrobatics of theoretical knowledge, without Ahriman, without ahrimanizing, without the condescending smile that has become customary meanwhile in our circles.

That is how Steiner spoke, and so, too, his student Michael Bauer. "Thou art our letter, written in our heart," says the apostle. Without the language of the heart — silence.

The Doctor and the Christ theme: In the end, everything that he has said leads toward the theme of Christus. All the gifts he brought to unfolding are, with infinite reverence, offered up to the Christ theme. The multiform unfolding of anthroposophical culture is Steiner's "silence." The Doctor traveling from city to city — the Doctor who builds bridges from the social question to art, from art to natural science, from there to the tasks of pedagogy — is the Doctor who is silent concerning the essential. This culture is a brilliant tapestry of outlooks, of vistas that can cause dizziness. One cannot help but ask, "Is all this splendor meant to be a field for man's activity?" A kind of future "culture-bearer" comes to mind — the lord of nature, the king, offering up the gifts of knowledge in a vessel. But then one comprehends the silence when it comes to the essential. The perspectives of cultural epochs — the word of his words, his word of the Logos; the gifts, the garments, the glory, all this is not destined for the human ego: "Not I, but Christ in me." Already the written word "*ich*"[30] is the monogram "I.CH." The human being — ruler and king — offers up the fruits of cultural development at the manger. Rulership and kingship are not the goal in themselves; the Doctor with his gifts is a finger pointing to the manger; and the Doctor bows before it.

When he spoke about the miracle of culture, the secrets of history and the mysteries, he seemed a "Magus," purple-clad, partaking of secrets. In that moment when all the gifts have been gathered together, the word "ich" resounds, but almost simultaneously: "Ich" becomes "I.CH.," becomes Jesus Christ. Higher powers guide the king and ruler of this world ... the primeval image is that of the high priesthood. Put everything together, all that has been said of the cultural epochs, of the human ego, and consider it all in the light of what has been said about the Christ. It signifies the transformation of the king and sage into humblest worship; the human being, wise man and king, offers up the splendor of selfhood at the manger. The human being becomes a shepherd!

When Rudolf Steiner spoke about the Christ, we were witnesses to the mystery of transformation of sage into shepherd. When he spoke about the Christ, he was a shepherd; when he spoke about the mystery cultures enwoven in the tapestry of cultural evolution, he was a wise man and if, on other occasions, one wanted to rebel against the Doctor or to doubt him — when he spoke about the Christ, his innermost hidden countenance was revealed: that of a shepherd. He, so widely admired, so readily "crowned" by the throng, stood there powerless, and himself laid the "I," the self, at the feet of newborn truth.

With this I try to characterize the tone of his statements concerning the Christ, statements that grew out of silence, and permeated the statements pertaining to the evolution of culture. Standing upon the summit of his magical interpretation of man's entire history, he revealed with utmost precision the magical, mystical viewpoints of history, and he did this, so to speak, kneeling. The unveiled foundation of history is revealed as the receptive womb of the Sophia, of Mary, of the soul who gives birth to the child. The helplessness of this child in his first earthly moments, the child who triumphs over might and force, and over Lucifer and Ahriman, was described by the Doctor in Berlin at Christmas, 1912, in a manner hardly possible to recount.

I recall the words, and call up before me the Doctor's countenance while he uttered these words. The defenselessness of the shepherd — who only through his love for the Child, in whose starry glory he stands, overcomes this helplessness — mirrored itself on the Doctor's countenance. He himself was like a child, that in its utter openness and vulnerability is immune to all temptations. Never will I forget him, a wise man who had surrendered himself to a child and had become a shepherd — simple, humble and filled with love. I see him above the speaker's rostrum — below him the roses — with a white, white, white face, a foreign whiteness, a luminousness that was no longer refracted color. Never before had I ever imagined, much less seen, such a white pure light. A warm purple glow streamed out from the Christ-permeated words. In this moment, it was not the "leader" or "transmitter" of the Christ impulse who stood before us. The "transmitter" is still a symbol, a chalice, a vessel, a something, that bears the impulse, that builds a riverbed in which it can flow.

But he who stood before us on that unforgettable evening — the 26th of December, 1912 — whose bearing, whose smile, was not meant for us but for an invisible center, the manger, that had arisen in our midst — could no longer be the mediator, because ability, strength, power — all these were inappropriate concepts. What they designate transformed itself into an actually incarnated something that was no longer the source of impulses but simply a presence, a single gesture of wonder, joy and love — a something that all its surroundings rushed to meet, strove to penetrate, and so were transformed thereby. The common conception of the sun is that of a disc, from which outraying spears of light break forth in all directions from the center to the periphery. Now, one must picture the counterimage. In the center — nothing; and the points of the periphery — people and objects — no longer remain themselves, but transform themselves to rays and pour as spears of light into what is abstractly called "center," but what in reality is not "center" but is the wholeness, the totality in which the Doctor and we, all of us, are one white sun of love for the Child.

Or, to use another analogy: all of us, clad in glistening garments, offer up our gifts, and he who gave them to us so that we might offer them up, stands there with empty hands — a defenseless shepherd — and bows and, helpless, only stirs, prods us to marvel: "There! Look Who lies there, Who is entrusted to us in all his vulnerability, whose defenselessness it is that brings victory over Lucifer and Ahriman! A single moment filled with the love for the Child makes the battle with Ahriman a thing of the past; where there is such love, there is victory." All this his gesture said when he interpreted the Gospel of St. Luke to us. Such a white radiance of light as enfolded him then, I have never before seen, nor even imagined. The words of Revelation came to my mind:

To him who conquers I will give a white stone, with a new name written on the stone which no one knows except him who receives it.

Oh, this peace-filled white light at rest within itself – of stillness! Only once, when I saw the white Starets of Sarov, the longing for it touched me, and now I felt the same wafting in the air; but this wafting did not come from the Doctor, though it was he who, through inner effort, made possible this moment.

The long silence, the fasting, the desert into which he withdrew, into which he had already called us, wordlessly and long before this moment, contributed to my carrying this lecture with me throughout my whole life as a moment filled with grace. Later, I often had to listen to how the word "grace" was misused; for instance, in a remark that the Doctor's "teachings" were "not blessed with grace." "Safeguard what has been entrusted to you, and avoid loose worldly chatter and the squabble of falsely praised art!" I thought, and saw before me the Doctor during the lecture of that 26th of December.

Before that and afterwards, he was silent on the theme of "Christ." The lectures between October and December dealt with other problems. ...

A few days after this lecture, for me so decisive, we heard the cycle *The Bhagavad Gita and the Epistles of St. Paul* in Cologne. It was a commentary fraught with significance, a tribute of acknowledgement and admiration for the East. It was an appreciation of India, contrasted with the characteristics of the apostle Paul, accentuating the imbalance of the "quarrelsome" Paul, who appeared after the glorious unfolding of the far more balanced and harmonious wisdom cultures of India. It was an indication of the transformation of the learned scribe and sage in Paul, who loses the balance and develops the shepherd-love of the Christian human being. In his "weakness" Paul leads into the future of love in the sense of St. John. ...

The theme of the Gospel of St. Luke resounded within me once again during Christmas of 1915, in Dornach, in connection with the Oberufer Christmas plays. Two different mysteries, two different stories, were presented on the stage. In one, the eerie one, the Wise Men from the East appeared, as did Herod and the Devil; in the other, the shepherds in the field. The lecture proceeded from the second play. Again, during the lecture, the same guileless warmth and gentleness revealed itself: the countenance of the shepherd. The Doctor spoke about the "owner" and the "shepherds."[31] The owner — the innkeeper — turns Mary and Joseph away from his door. Mary gives birth in a stable to which the shepherds come. Two human types become apparent: the "owner" or innkeeper, and the "donor," the shepherd, who protects the soul from egotism, regardless of the form in which it may appear. The Doctor called upon us to worship at the manger with the Child, humbly like the shepherds.

So his countenance appeared as he contemplated the Jesus Child, the one who was the chalice into which the Logos poured itself. The childlike clarity united in his features with a suffering that I cannot describe and before which all words fail. Only a person who suffered as the Doctor did could, in some instances, be a pure-white little child. And later on also — when he spoke about Jesus of Nazareth, who hid himself away in a carpenter's shop until his thirtieth year and knew a suffering never before known by any living person — there shone behind the pain, the same modest smile. With a hesitant, almost embarrassed smile, the Doctor also said that Jesus bore a mark upon his face; and when we beheld the mark, we began to love Jesus. The dying embers of the melting pain before which all suffering paled, awoke our love; this pain exercised a gentle force of attraction upon us.

The theme of unspoiled love wove itself into the theme of inexpressible suffering. Through inexpressible innocent suffering, the Child was to become a chalice for the Logos, who in turn took upon Himself a different, equally innocent suffering for the sake of the whole world. Jesus' suffering in seeing his fellow men possessed by devils crossed itself with the anguish of Christ, Who innocently took upon Himself the horror and pain of self-constriction into the personality of Jesus. This cross of suffering forms the basis for the three-year-long biography of Christ Jesus. Christ submerged into the personality of Jesus; Jesus, borne aloft by the Christ force, became Jesus Christ.

The Doctor pointed to the cross of twofold suffering, to the agonies in both relations: Jesus Christ and Christ Jesus. Before its union with the Logos, the personality of Jesus experienced the black hole of the world within the center of his "I," his ego: the world abyss, a concept commensurate with that of the Copernican universe. Jesus prior to the baptism — an "It," over which the Ahriman-emptied universe is torn asunder. So this "It" went to the baptism — under the double cross of "Jesus Christ" — while the "Christ," Who in freedom had left the realm of spirit-light in order to be drawn into the narrow hole of personality, had to endure the horror and pain of an incomparable constriction, beside which any form of insanity would be — a nothing. He had to endure this torture so as to become "Christ Jesus," so that He could live within Jesus.

Two crosses: "Jesus Christ," "Christ Jesus." The moment of the baptism in the Jordan: the realization of both crosses in one cross — the cross on Golgotha — the concrete process of Christ's being born into the earth. Steiner points to the crossing of two paths of suffering — never before pointed out — that merge into a third. For the first time, he points to the cross on Golgotha from a vantage point that even remained hidden to the apostles: as a shaking to the foundations of divine and human destiny. "Gods" and "Men" must perish in order to arise to a new potential, not only human and not only divine, that justifies everything that is — not only the humanness of man but also the divinity of God. The new form of life, the only possible form, now still only a seed, will in the future be concretely born, a sign of the incarnation of "this" into "that" and of "that" into "this": Christ Jesus and the world, "I" and nature, "Spirit" and history and theory.

When Steiner spoke about Jesus Christ, the love for the defenseless Child reverberated in his words. But when he spoke about the Christ — chaste glowing pain, suffering born of love, love born of suffering crossed one another, in his words.

No one has brought about anything similar to what Rudolf Steiner gave rise to when, for the souls of human beings, he developed his Christology. Here was no knowledge in the ordinary sense of the word. It was a love overflowing all forms, a suffering overflowing all forms.

The mark that he bore on his countenance at such a time, "*Ich,*" was an expression of his state of consciousness that awoke the listeners from their sleep.

He stood before us in stern silence, in the outer court of his words on the Christ.

Head of Christ from statue, Representative of Humanity.

Glimpses of the Building of the First Goetheanum and the Start of the World War

Sonia Tomara Clark and Jeannette Eaton

The following passage is taken from the manuscript of an unpublished book about Rudolf Steiner.

Living in a fool's paradise and enjoying a high level of prosperity, the peoples of Europe in the years immediately preceding the first World War seemed to have no inkling of the destructive forces which such a conflict would unleash. Steiner was perhaps one of the few whose penetrating mind could read the future and embrace the magnitude of the danger hanging over the old continent. He was fully aware of the changes it might bring in its wake. Desperately he tried to warn his contemporaries of the follies of nationalistic adventures.

What a relief he felt when he returned from long journeys to the Dornach hill. Already a number of men and women had gathered to help with the building. Roads had been constructed above the village and a large workshop, the Schreinerei, had been built. Some 150 men were at work — swarthy Italian masons and tall blond carpenters from the wharfs of Hamburg. Rudolf Steiner found that students of his from many countries had come to Dornach ready to undertake whatever he might call on them to do. One of them later described the group:

> "Smart American women, a Russian who wears an enormous fur hat, a musician with a grass green umbrella, ladies with short-cropped hair — all these people wander happily through the soft red clay which engulfs our rubber boots beyond retrieving. ... A common effort has brought us together from East and West. We are not experienced builders; only a few of us are sculptors by profession. But with good will one can learn fast. ..."

In March, 1914, Dr. Steiner came for an unusually long stay in order to show his friends how to carve the capitals of the great wooden pillars destined to support the ceilings of the two halls. One collaborator, Assia Turgenieff, a Russian artist, sketched this word picture:

> "The person most frequently met on this hill was Dr. Steiner. Wearing a workman's smock and high boots, he hurried from one workshop to another, a model or sketchbook in his hand, he stopped on his way with a friendly word or a handshake. ..."

And her sister, Nathalie Turgenieff-Pozzo, gave a detailed picture of the carving lessons.[32]

> "The first day of woodcarving has come; we have before us a row of wooden blocks more than a yard each in height and width. Dr. Steiner has provided us with small models which we are to copy. We take chisels and mallets. A great effort is needed to cut even a splinter out of tile block. We take counsel, we pull on the wood, we are already tired. Our arms are sore, yet one sees no result of the effort.

> "Dr. Steiner comes on the second day, takes a mallet and a chisel, climbs on a wooden crate and begins to work. He too has never done such work before, but after a few blows with the mallet he appears to be quite familiar with it and cuts one furrow after another. We see him hammer for ten minutes, one hour, two hours, without stopping. We stand at a distance, pale with exhaustion, and look at him in awed silence. We knew by experience how hard the work was. ..."

To this her sister Assia added:

> "He was completely absorbed in his work, as if he studied inwardly the movements of his hands, as if he listened to something whispered out of the wood. ..."

Both by example and specific directions, Steiner taught his amateur carvers. He teased them merrily, amused them with anecdotes, encouraged their efforts, paid no heed to their weariness and in the evening gathered them all into the workshop to hear one of his profound and inspiring lectures. By April 1st the great domes, covered with Norwegian slate, were in place and a roofing celebration was held. Architects giving Dr. Steiner technical help had warned him that his plan for the two intersecting domes which were to support one another, could not be realized, that the domes would collapse. But there they were, in perfect balance, firm as rocks. It was heartwarming to observe Steiner's glowing pleasure in this result.

Doubtless he would have loved to settle down in Dornach to watch every slight advancement of the building's construction. Practical activity delighted him. He welcomed visitors as early as eight o'clock in the morning, but two hours later he was usually in the building yards. Then he painted, modeled, carved, interrupted often by questions from architects or workmen. He never failed to attend Fräulein von Sivers' eurythmy and dramatic rehearsals. Every evening he gave a lecture to the volunteers. A few hours of sleep were sufficient to restore his forces.

Yet even when joyously at work, Steiner found it hard to forget the threat of conflict. His understanding encompassed all countries. He was a citizen of the world. So for weeks he toured Vienna, Prague, Paris and Scandinavia, in addition to visiting many German cities. It was almost midsummer when he returned to Dornach.

The end of June brought the shocking news of the assassination in Bosnia of the Archduke Franz Ferdinand, heir to the Imperial throne of Austria-Hungary. Vienna was stunned and excitement spread through the Imperial palace, where the Serbian government was held responsible for the crime. Well-informed, thoughtful persons like Rudolf Steiner feared that this whole situation might be the spark that would start a conflagration in Europe. But several weeks passed without definite signs of a blaze.

A small party from Basel had planned to go to Bayreuth to hear Wagner's opera *Parsifal* and both Dr. Steiner and Fräulein von Sivers joined it. As the train reached the station of Bayreuth, a roar of men's voices arose from the platform and a troop of soldiers rushed cheering through the train. No one knew exactly what the demonstration meant, but feared it marked the mobilization of the German army. Such was the prelude to *Parsifal*.

At the opera's end a friend offered to take the Dornach party to Mannheim, nearer to the Swiss border. A large automobile was waiting to drive her to that city for a farewell to her two sons. It was a wild trip. At every bridge the shout of "Halt!" from a guard stopped the travelers who were obliged to show identification papers. On through the night the car plunged.

A dense crowd was waiting at the Mannheim station for the train to Basel. It did not arrive until nearly morning. Above groans of fatigue arose hysterical cries: "It's war now! No mistake about it!" Marie von Sivers said of Steiner: "The expression of grief on his face was almost unbearable."

Soon thereafter the group of workers on Dornach's hill heard the dull, distant roar of mighty guns, a sound which was never to cease for four dreadful years.

The immediate effect of the war's outbreak upon the anthroposophical center was crushing. Most of the men busy on the building, whether artists or laborers, had to leave at once. Even the Swiss were called away for border patrol to protect the neutrality of their country. Some of the women departed to help their families or serve the Red Cross. Hardly half the group was left.

Rudolf Steiner accepted these decisions without word or gesture to reveal what this exodus meant to his plans. Instead his farewell message was: "The only thing I can say is that everyone must do his duty." He was grateful for the nucleus of workers who remained. Representatives of seventeen countries, many of which were already fighting each other, gladly joined together to serve the cause of Anthroposophy.

To them Steiner said with quiet force: "Our work must go on." Yet well he knew that nothing — nothing — would ever be the same again.

A Student's Memories of Rudolf Steiner

Lisa Dreher Monges

It was a great good fortune that allowed me to meet Rudolf Steiner for the first time when I was five years old. In 1908, my mother, Frau Paula Dreher, had become a member of the German Section of the Theosophical Society that was under the direction of Dr. Steiner, and in Stuttgart in 1911, shortly after the dedication of the new home of the Theosophical Society in the Landhausstrasse 70, my mother had an appointment with Dr. Steiner. She took me along and introduced me to him. While I do not remember the events immediately before or after this occasion, I clearly remember the occasion itself, which took place in the so-called Blue Room of the newly dedicated house: Dr. Steiner's slender figure of medium height, his black hair, his black eyes, his dark suit and black flowing silk tie; and even today I can feel the kindness that flowed from him to me as he took my hand and put his other hand on my head.

It was again my great good fortune to become one of the first pupils of the original Waldorf School in Stuttgart which, in 1919, was founded by my uncle, Emil Molt, and which was under the direction of Rudolf Steiner. I was at that time in the 7th grade (the Waldorf School had eight grades from the very beginning) and was thus able, to a certain extent, to realize the importance that was attached to the founding of this school under the spiritual guidance of Rudolf Steiner.

The school was dedicated on September 7, 1919 in the great hall of the Stuttgart Stadtgarten. Emil Molt spoke the opening words of greeting. Then Rudolf Steiner addressed the assembled future teachers, students, and the latter's parents, who were mostly the employees and workers of Emil Molt's Waldorf Astoria Cigarette factory, and some members of the Anthroposophical Society. Rudolf Steiner described the basis and aims of the pedagogy to be practiced in this school. A few weeks prior to this dedication festival, a group of children, among them my sister Dora and myself, had eurythmy with the Ur-eurythmist, Lory Maier-Smits. Eurythmy, as an art, was then just seven years old. In the eurythmy program performed after Dr. Steiner's dedication address, we did rod exercises, and, together with the adult eurythmists, some humoresques by Christian Morgenstern. Rudolf Steiner was present at the rehearsals, which were under the direction of Marie Steiner — she also recited the texts in the program — and during the dress rehearsal he came up onto the stage, took the eurythmy copper rods and showed the tallest girl among us how she should hold them on her arms and how we, with a slight bend toward her, should receive them. Rudolf Steiner called this occasion of the Waldorf School a "Festival Act in the History of Mankind."

Many vivid and precious pictures of Rudolf Steiner's frequent visits to the Waldorf School and to our classrooms during the next five years up to his last illness arise before the eye of the soul. I shall try to describe some that are most characteristic. It was a time of glowing enthusiasm, of joy and gratitude for all that we children received from Rudolf Steiner and our teachers, it was the happiest time of my life and shines forth in my memory in a golden glow. Dr. Steiner had directed that on every first Thursday of the month there should take place a so-called *Monatsfeier* (monthly festival), in which the whole school gathered in the assembly hall, and the various grades showed what they had learned in foreign languages, recitation, eurythmy, singing, and so forth. Very often Dr. Steiner was present at these festivals and addressed, first, the younger pupils, then us older ones, and finally the teachers. I remember his great delight when, at the very first of these festivals, a little boy in the first grade gave him a washrag he had knitted for him. The little boy had a typically Swabian name: *Häfele* (Little Pot). Dr. Steiner held up the washrag and said, *"Euer lieber guter Häfele hat mir einen Waschlappen gestrickt. Mit dem soll ich mich nun jeden Tag waschen."* ("Your dear, good little Häfele has knitted me a washrag, and now I will wash myself with it every day.") Then he continued: "Dear children, just as we have to keep our bodies clean, so we must see to it that we keep our souls pure and clean."

At another monthly festival Dr. Steiner spoke to us of two wings which every child must develop. He said: "We have no wings to fly in the air with like the birds, but we can grow two wings, one on the right side, one on the left. The one on the right side is diligence, the other on the left, attentiveness. If we develop these wings, we shall become industrious and capable human beings (*tüchtige Menschen*) who can fly with them into life."

Dr. Steiner invariably ended his addresses to us children with the question: "Do you love your teachers?" ("*Habt ihr eure Lehrer lieb?*" to which we answered, out of the full conviction of our hearts, with a strong, loud "Yes!") One time, after the summer vacation, Dr. Steiner spoke to the assembled children on the first day of the new school year. As he came to the end of his address we expected to hear him ask the familiar question and we were inwardly ready for the familiar and joyful answer. This time, however, he asked: "Did you not forget your teachers?" Now we could not shout "*Ja!*" This required another answer. The whole group of about a thousand children hesitated for a moment. Dr. Steiner made an encouraging gesture with both arms, and finally we broke into a loud "*Nein!*" How different was the experience of a convinced answer in the negative from the accustomed one in the affirmative!

An unforgettable picture: Rudolf Steiner walking across the schoolyard, surrounded by countless children, the little ones literally hanging on his arms and legs like grapes on a vine, he struggling to get his arms free to be able to shake hands with us older students.

Dr. Steiner visited the various grades of the school from time to time. It was always a tremendous joy for us — our hearts began "to beat higher" — when the door of the classroom suddenly opened and Rudolf Steiner walked in. We rose from our seats, and Dr. Steiner greeted us with both arms raised up high. He listened to what the teacher was teaching, and very often he took up the thread and continued to teach where the teacher had left off. One day he entered our room — I think we were then in the ninth grade — and said rather sternly: "Something is wrong in this classroom!" I wondered what he could mean, and then I discovered that there was the wrong date on the calendar hanging on the wall. I raised my hand and said so, and Dr. Steiner walked over, without saying anything further, and with a decided motion pulled off the page with the wrong date. We had sat in that room for about two hours without discovering that the calendar had not been brought "up to date," but Dr. Steiner saw it the moment he entered the room!

During a lesson in the History of Art Dr. Steiner told us: "When you take all the colors that Leonardo da Vinci used in his Last Supper, put them on a disk and rotate this disk very fast, you will get the color white. But if you take the colors of the figures of Christ and of Judas Iscariot and mix them together, you will get the color grey."

A most memorable experience was the laying of the foundation stone for the new main building of the Waldorf School by Dr. Steiner in December, 1921. Students, teachers, Rudolf Steiner, Marie Steiner, Emil Molt (the founder of the school), Berta Molt, the architect Weippert, officers of the Waldorf School Association and friends of the school were assembled in the large eurythmy hall in the so-called 'barrack'. Dr. Steiner addressed the assembly and read his words which were written on a parchment tablet, signed by him, and all those mentioned above, as well as by the teachers. These words described the aims and purpose of the activities to be carried on in the newly-to-be-erected building and ended with the following three lines:

> With pure intentions
> And good will
> In the name of Jesus Christ.

It was a deeply moving experience to hear Dr. Steiner pronounce these words and then see him place the parchment in a pentagon-dodecahedron of copper which was then immediately sealed and carried out onto the building site where it was lowered into a concrete slab which was then also sealed. Dr. Steiner took a hammer and with it struck the concrete slab three times. Then he did the same on behalf of Marie Steiner. After this the founder of the school, all the teachers and every single child in turn carried out the same act.

This foundation stone escaped destruction when, 23 years later, the building was destroyed in a bombing attack in World War II, and today it still rests under the entrance steps of the now re-erected building.

At Christmas, 1922, I was invited to spend the holidays with a friend and her mother and sister at the Goetheanum in Dornach. I accepted this invitation with great joy. Thus, I was able, evening after evening, to hear

Dr. Steiner's lectures in the great hall of the Goetheanum. The public lecture cycle's title was *Der Entstehungs-moment der Naturwissenschaft in der Weitgeschichte und ihre seithenge Entwicklung* (*The Birth of Natural Science in World History and its Development*). Dr. Steiner stood on a platform, surrounded by the beautiful forms of the speaker's podium, in the center of the space before the closed curtain, behind which was the stage and the small cupola. His deep and warm voice sounded forth in harmony with all forms of the fourteen pillars, the architraves, the paintings in the large cupola and the pictures that were etched into the colored windows.

I do not recall the content of the lectures, but Dr. Steiner's gestures as he was speaking I remember well. When he spoke one of his long sentences, he accompanied it with a weaving movement of his arms and hands. Or he would concentrate his gestures or widen his arms, even slightly shaking the fingers when the statement he was making came to a climax, and this was followed by an all-embracing movement of both arms with the conclusion of the statement. Two years later, when Dr. Steiner first gave the eurythmy gestures for the musical intervals, it dawned upon me that these and Dr. Steiner's gestures when lecturing had the same origin. I do not say that Dr. Steiner carried out eurythmy gestures when he lectured, but these movements all sprang from the same source.

On December 31st, on New Year's Eve at five o'clock, a eurythmy performance was given on the great stage of the Goetheanum. As was his custom, Dr. Steiner spoke some introductory words before this performance, the first part of which was the "Prologue in Heaven" from Goethe's Faust. Dr. Steiner stood in front of the closed curtain somewhat to the right of the center of the stage. As he spoke, there was a moment of tension, of danger, when suddenly in the center and front of the stage, and directly to the left of Dr. Steiner as seen from the audience, the big trap door opened in the floor. Out of this, during the performance, Mephisto was to rise in the "Prologue in Heaven." Dr. Steiner seemed to be unaware of the sudden deep, gaping hole right next to him. Luckily, young Graf von Polzer-Hoditz had the presence of mind to jump up onto the stage, take hold of Dr. Steiner's arm and lead him away from the danger spot. Dr. Steiner seemed to be astonished at this sudden action, but as he looked to the side, he must have seen in what danger he had been. Two steps to the side, and he would have fallen into the gaping hole. He continued his introduction without interruption.

The performance itself, on the great Goetheanum stage, was beautiful beyond words. The "Prologue in Heaven," surrounded by the twelve carved pillars and the paintings above in the small dome — it was really heaven.

At eight o'clock, New Year's Eve, Dr. Steiner gave a lecture, *The Spiritual Communion of Mankind*, in the great hall of the Goetheanum. This was strictly a members' lecture. One had to be eighteen years old to become a member, and since my friend and I were lacking one year, we did not attend. Instead, a group of us young people met at the Villa Duldeck[33], the home of Dr. Grosheintz, which Dr. Steiner had designed, and we decided to stay up till midnight for a New Year's Eve party. I lived, with the friend who had invited me, in a room in the house of a family down the hill in Dornach-Brugg. At around half past nine o'clock, we walked past the Goetheanum where we met the night watchman with his German shepherd watchdog making the rounds. We greeted one another; everything was peaceful and quiet as we walked down the hill to tell our landlord that we would not get home till after midnight. Then we turned around and started back up the hill. When we were halfway up to the Goetheanum, a lady came running toward us, calling out: "The Goetheanum is on fire!" We could not believe our ears but ran up the hill as fast as we could. Grey smoke was pouring out of the upper windows of the south wing of the Goetheanum and crawling like snakes over the silvery slate roof. It was about ten o'clock at night by then. There were calls for water, so we joined a chain of helpers, filling the buckets in the Schreinerei and handing them along the line. Oh, how slowly the water ran out of the faucet. Then there were calls from the terrace: "Bring ladders!" There were a few ladders lying near the Schreinerei. I grabbed one and rushed with it as fast as I could through the south portal and up the concrete stairs that led to the stage and dressing rooms. I could not get very far, for the space was filled with transparent, greenish smoke which made breathing impossible. I started to cough and could have suffocated. A Russian eurythmist came running after me and pulled me down the stairs. I had to abandon the ladder.

In the meantime the firemen and fire engines from Dornach had arrived. Dr. Steiner gave the order that everybody should leave the Goetheanum. The firemen took over. We were asked to fetch vinegar to help the men who had suffered from smoke inhalation. So a friend and I ran down to Haus Eckinger and brought up what vinegar we could find there for the first aid station which Frau Kolisko had put up in the meadow near Haus de Jaager.

The clouds of smoke became thicker and thicker as they crawled now over both cupolas. One could hear the crackling of the fire, but no flames were visible. The Goetheanum had double walls, an inner and outer wall with air space between them. The two cupolas also were double — an inner one on which were the paintings, and an outer one covered with silvery Norwegian slate. There was quite a bit of space between them. Through this space, between the walls and between the domes, the fire ate its way. One could not see it from outside.

Suddenly, as the church bells of Dornach and Arlesheim pealed the hour of midnight and rang in the New Year, a tremendous flame burst forth where the two domes met. Now it was clear that there was no help. Piece by piece, the large and the small dome collapsed. Now the firemen directed the streams of water onto the Schreinerei, the carpentry shop. The heat was tremendous. The water rose up as steam from the roof. We carried out all the books from the bookstore, which was in one wing of the Schreinerei, down into Haus de Jaager. We managed loads we would not have been able to carry under ordinary circumstances.

And there, near his studio which contained his great wooden sculpture — the Christ between Lucifer and Ahriman — stood Dr. Steiner gazing into the raging fire, on his right Miss Maryon, the sculptress, on his left Fräulein Waller. I stood quite near to them as someone came running up to Dr. Steiner and told him that some members were trying to move the Christ statue from his studio out onto the meadow behind the Schreinerei. Dr. Steiner said that should not be done and sent Fräulein Waller to give the message. She came too late; they had already moved the statue.

The fire made its murderous progress. First the two domes collapsed; then the walls were swallowed by the flames, the big windows melting in the tremendous heat. Then the north and south wings caved in; the west wing was the last to go. When the flames engulfed the organ pipes located in the west of the great hall, they responded with strange musical sounds. The flames took on all manner of colors as they melted the great metal pipes. Now nothing remained but two circles: one of fourteen columns, the other of twelve, They stood like flaming torches in the black night sky, a sight both of horror and beauty. One by one they fell over into the concrete substructure where the fire continued to burn for two more days.

Thick smoke rose above the flames. "It cannot be!" we said to ourselves as we gazed at the billowing smoke above the concrete foundation. "Surely, the smoke will clear away and the Goetheanum will be there in all its beauty." Alas, there before us was only gaping, physical nothingness.

The Schreinerei was saved through the efforts of the firemen. But the water had flooded the rooms behind the stage, and now the floors had to be dried, for Dr. Steiner had asked that the Conference go on as scheduled for New Year's Day, in the Schreinerei: at 5 P.M., the *Three Kings Play*; at 8 P.M., his lecture in the series on *The Birth of Natural Science*. Everybody helped to get the Schreinerei ready for the five o'clock performance, which then took place as scheduled, while over at the Goetheanum site the fire was still flaming.

The curtain of the Schreinerei stage opened; the Angel, played by Ina Schuurman, stepped forward and, speaking the first words of greeting in the Austrian dialect of the plays, "*I tritt herei an oilen spot, a schen guatn abend geb eng God.*" ("I enter here joyfully and bid you from God a beautiful good evening"), her voice failed her, and she fought back her tears. After a short struggle, she gained the victory over the pain that gripped the hearts of all of us who had experienced this terrible night, this unheard-of disaster; she ended her speech and the play went on without mishap.

For Dr. Steiner's lecture at eight o'clock the audience had assembled early and sat in the Schreinerei hall in complete silence, waiting for him, If, on other occasions, one had seen him walking up the Goetheanum hill, one was impressed by his light and forward-striving step. One might call it an iambic step — without heaviness. Dr. Steiner and Frau Doktor had a room behind the Schreinerei stage; and now, as we all sat there in silence, waiting, we heard heavy steps approaching, the feet dragging; and Dr.

Steiner entered through the blue curtain beside the stage and stepped to the speaker's desk. We all rose and stood in reverence before this great and beloved human being. Dr. Steiner, with a voice of deepest sadness, as one mortally wounded, spoke a few sentences about the great loss we had experienced: "*Das Liebe Goetheanum, zehn Jahre Arbeit.*" ("The dear Goetheanum, ten years of work.") And then, with unbroken strength, he gave his lecture.

A year later, in his lecture of December 31, 1923, Dr. Steiner said that in the flames of the burning temple of Artemis at Ephesus one could read the envy of the Gods; in the flames of the burning Goetheanum one could read the envy of human beings.

There remains with me as precious memories the lunches at the house of Emil and Berta Molt, at which Rudolf Steiner and Marie Steiner were present and I was allowed to participate. Dr. Steiner wished a joyful mood to prevail during mealtimes, and while dessert was served, he frequently told jokes.

It was in February, 1924, that Rudolf Steiner and Marie Steiner came to lunch at Haus Molt for the last time. The lively conversation had turned to automobiles and to Henry Ford, and Rudolf Steiner said that he liked to ride in a Ford car (it was the "Model T" of that time). He continued: "Henry Ford has just published his memoirs," and jokingly he added: "Many people have 'memoiritis' nowadays," upon which Marie Steiner remarked: "That can be said of you, too," for Rudolf Steiner was at that time writing his autobiography which appeared, week after week, in the periodical Das Goetheanum. As Frau Doktor made this remark, Dr. Steiner's facial expression changed to deep seriousness. He looked up, his black eyes seemed to gaze into far distances, and he said with his deep and resounding, warm voice, very slowly: "*Ja, es soll nur schlicht und wahr sein.*" ("Yes, but it must be only simple and true.") After a short pause, Emil Molt said: "One ought to write Frau Doktor's biography, too." Whereupon Dr. Steiner replied: "*Das kann man ja nicht. Frau Doktor ist ein kosmisches Wesen.*" ("That cannot be done. Frau Doktor is a cosmic being.")[34]

The last time I saw Rudolf Steiner, he was lying on his deathbed in his studio in the Schreinerei at the Goetheanum, at the feet of the Christ statue which he himself had carved. The soft candlelight threw a golden glow over his beloved countenance, which bore the expression of greatest love as though he were going to open his eyes any moment and utter words of kindness. The fragrance of countless flowers pervaded the room. Among them was a wreath fashioned of every imaginable flower from garden and meadow sent by the children of the Waldorf School who had lost their greatest teacher and friend whom they loved like a father. Another wreath of red roses, sent by Albert Steffen, bore the inscription:

Dem Gottesfreund und Menschheitsführer
Rudolf Steiner
(To the Friend of God and Leader of Mankind, Rudolf Steiner).

A great number of people had gathered for the cremation at the cemetery in Basel. Only few found room inside the crematorium, which was a much smaller building than the present one. Most people had to stand outside during the funeral service, among them my mother and myself. Through the open door one could hear clearly what went on inside. First there sounded the funeral music composed by Jan Stuten. Then Dr. Rittelmeyer carried out the funeral service. After that Albert Steffen spoke, and music concluded the service. As Marie Steiner, Albert Steffen, Dr. Wegmann, Dr. Vreede, and Dr. Wachsmuth left the crematorium and came down the steps, the smoke began to rise from the chimney. The spring sun radiated, and suddenly there appeared a flock of white birds: it rose in spirals with the smoke and disappeared into the blue of the heavens. [35]

Impressions of a Young American Student

Arvia MacKaye Ege

As one of a small group of college students, I had the good fortune to spend the summer of 1923 traveling in Europe. We had been sent over by a student organization which had become interested in the Youth Movement so widespread at that time particularly in Germany, in order to learn through first-hand experience about its ideals and aims, and during our travels we came in contact with groups of young people of the most varied interests and activities.

When we reached southern Germany, I realized that my chance had come to hear and meet a man of whom I had been told much that interested me from a friend, Irene Brown, an artist who was a cousin of both Albert Spaulding, the violinist, and of Scott Pyle, the painter. So, leaving my companions temporarily, I set off alone with my knapsack on my back for Dornach, Switzerland, where I had been told he carried on his work.

At length, I found myself climbing a steep Swiss hillside dotted with tiny cottages, a ruined castle high above, until I came upon a simple outdoor eating place with rough benches and tables. After making some inquiry, a kindly English lady took me under her wing, and in a short time I was seated among several hundred people in a large wooden building further up the hill. Here, a slight figure in a somewhat worn, black frock coat, rose and walked to a speaker's desk at the right of a blue curtain which apparently hid a stage where a performance was about to begin. There was gravity in his step. He walked and stood with an erect carriage of the head and shoulders which immediately gave a sense of power to his otherwise rather delicate build. His wide forehead and the deep, penetrating gaze of his eyes, the rhythm of his gestures as he began to speak and the resonance of his voice awakened my interest and confidence. His words seemed to flow out of a fullness quite beyond my grasp, yet as I listened his simplicity and warmth amazed me.

This was Rudolf Steiner, a unique figure in Europe at that time, author and lecturer, and a pioneer thinker of this century. He spoke only briefly, for a performance of eurythmy followed, forming in my recollection a background of lucid motion and color for the impression I have already described.

But my one encompassing memory of that afternoon was of the startling reality, the commanding depth of this man who spoke so simply here in a wooden barracks on a Swiss hillside. An immediacy of experience imbued his words and bearing with an extraordinary quality of life. And I remember so well as I ran down that steep hillside in the dark on my way back to rejoin my friends, saying to myself as my feet hit the ground – "I shall come back, no matter what happens!"

And I did return.

It was in late October 1923, that I saw Rudolf Steiner again.

Now I entered once more that wooden barracks, actually a carpentry shop known as the Schreinerei, as one of the gathering throng who trooped up the hill by various paths under the bright autumn stars, making our way past the charred ruins of a great building, to converge upon a small doorway of this weathered structure. The threshold and plank floor inside, worn by the tread of so many feet over their knotted surfaces, had taken on smooth, undulating forms, as though carved by the wash of the sea. Here to the right we hung our coats on racks among large band saws and workbenches and continued further past piles of lumber and shavings to a second doorway at the far end, the entrance to the improvised auditorium. It was a large room of rough wood with a low, double-peaked roof, built with two parallel ridgepoles and several shuttered skylights and must have seated about five- to six-hundred people. Across the end to the left was the raised stage, closed off with the blue curtains I remembered.

As the last latecomers found their seats, a door was heard to open and close backstage, followed by a sound of footsteps. Then at one side the folds of the curtain stirred and parted as Rudolf Steiner swung them aside and stepped through. There was a quiet air of ceaseless labor about him. With a smile of greeting and a certain unforgettable gesture which I came to know so well, a slight inclination of head and hand to one side as if in gracious deference to the friends about him, he walked to the speaker's stand at the center below the stage. His pace was measured, as if he carried his body forward with conscious effort, although at the same time there was a lightness, even eagerness about him. Yet once he was on the speaker's stand a complete calm fell about him. He stood for a moment in deep concentration – one strong hand clasped over the wrist of the other, his eyelids lowered, as if cloaked in a quiet so deep that it seemed to descend to primal foundations and there to draw breath. It was as if he were listening to the far reaches of the universe and the whole world paused to listen with him.

Then one by one, like drops from a subterranean spring, his words came clear and strong, slowly at first, then gradually increasing to a steady flow. Gestures began to accompany them. Strangely he now gave the impression of being of great stature, and as the content of his words unfolded, so his whole organism and being seemed to unfold with it. With the ease and naturalness with which a plant evolves, each movement, the expression of his face, his voice, took on an ever increasing life, form, rhythm, as they became a vehicle for the thoughts and images which he wove and built before his listeners.

Yet all of this did not take place in the realm of semi-dream, as is sometimes the case with a great artist. Neither was it the ordinary wide-awake world of the brilliant intellect. But the whole seemed steeped in the clarified sunlight of a super-awareness — a reality so immediate and instantaneous, so fresh and powerful, that the everyday soon seemed shadowy in comparison. It was as though you were suddenly shocked out of sleep to find yourself awake for a brief interval and to realize that most of your life you had been dreaming. Yet there was no tension, no pressure – only a great fullness, illumined and ordered by a stern clarity, which, while it warmed your heart, and gave wings to your soul, at the same time shook you to the roots of your being.

This impression occupied me so intensely that it was only with the greatest effort that I was gradually able to focus fully upon the content of what he was saying. My German, too, which was far from adequate, only added to the effort needed. But fortunately I had been steeped in the language for the whole summer and could at least follow the main thread of the thought.

Gradually, as I listened, a great tapestry was unfolded and painted before my inner eyes. The basic impression that lives with me, gathered through this and other lectures which I was to hear, is one of a majestic view of the relationship of man and universe. Man, the crown of nature, bears within himself the creative powers of evolution itself. Nature is a more or less finished product of the past; the human being alone harbors the forces of the future. What he makes his own, what he transforms and builds into the eternal kernel of his being, will exist even after the earth shall have passed away, as a part of the active spiritual forces of the universe. For just as there are kingdoms below man – animal, plant, mineral – so there are kingdoms above him, stages of consciousness higher than his own – spiritualities of far loftier awareness and creativity than his, whose outer works appear in the endless wonders of the cosmos, the earth and within man himself. He is the link between two realms – the crown of the one and the earthly threshold to the other. Preoccupied more and more exclusively with the former, he has been almost wholly unaware of the latter during recent centuries, and has lacked sufficient strength to reach up to it. Today, however, after the strict training of his powers of objective thought through natural science, which has given him a knowledge of the kingdoms below him, he has developed sufficient inward strength to acquire gradually an objective science of those kingdoms which can be found within and above him — a spiritual science — whereby he may become a conscious, creative participant in the course of evolution.

This is indeed not the exact content of what I heard on this occasion or during later lectures. But it is an intimation of the general import of what I now began to take in during the many times I was to hear Rudolf Steiner and those few opportunities when I was privileged to speak with him. As he lectured, describing and developing step by step an understanding of these realms, he seemed to become an instrument of them, to become young and powerful – to be, as it were, a musical accompaniment to the scope and magnitude of his words which carried his listeners into the hidden heart of things or out into the life of those realms which lie beyond the boundaries of time and space. Yet just as surely did he, at the end, bring them back and set them down with their feet squarely and firmly on the earth, there to meet the more forcefully the everyday tasks of the immediate present. With an acid truth, and through his uncompromising gravity and humor, he seemed to tear away unequivocally any possibility of sensationalism.

On this particular evening after the lecture, while people were standing about talking as the hall slowly emptied, I watched him as he talked with a small group of friends not far away, his head slightly inclined to one side listening. All at once he looked up, and his gaze met mine. It was like an objective ray of light, and I had the inescapable feeling that he looked directly at me and knew that I was there. I had the definite sense that he was aware of everything that went on about him, that he knew and had an intimate understanding for everyone present. This was a foolish exaggeration on my part, I told myself. Later, I was to find out that I was not alone in this experience. And when, a few minutes afterward, Irene Brown took me over and found it possible to introduce me to him, his greeting was such that I was convinced it was true. In that one handclasp and the warm directness of his gaze I felt recognized in my deepest strivings, and yet in a quite impersonal way that left me so free that it almost took my breath.

During the weeks that followed I would ask myself again and again – "Are you a complete fool? Have you lost all sense of proportion and fallen prey to a serious case of hero worship as many young women do? Or are you allowing yourself to be convinced of mere illusion?"

Again and again I would search myself and wrestle with the wealth of new ideas which were presented to me. I studied also a number of his books. Soon I realized that the essence of these books was a recognition and scrupulous regard for the freedom of the individual. Indeed, the very basis of free will – denied today by natural science – a philosophy of the free spiritual activity of the human being, was here laid down and firmly established for the first time in the history of human thinking. Nowhere was belief in authority appealed to or condoned, but a new vista of scientific thought was opened up, a "spiritual science," illuminating and enhancing natural science, and the methods whereby it was won, clearly and soberly shown.

It came over me gradually that I was taking part in a significant movement in history when, just as revolutionary discoveries — such as those in the field of electronics and of air travel, for instance — were taking place in the external world, even more revolutionary ones were being made in the interior, super-physical world of which human thought is only the borderline. Discoveries which, when actively recognized and taken in by men, would usher in a new era of human development.

Rudolf Steiner, 1879.

Here men and women of all walks of life — day laborers, countesses and businessmen — met in this recognition. And it did not take me very long before I had thoroughly convinced myself that I would indeed have to call myself a fool were I to consider these people all mad and to close my mind to the host of new thoughts which I encountered here.

Not long after this, when I was not occupied with my studies and new household duties – caring for the little adopted son of Irene Brown – I took the opportunity of investigating the ruins of the great building which lay at the brink of the hill, just below and in front of the Schreinerei. The concrete foundations comprising the lower story, or basement, were still standing, all that now remained of the great structure called the Goetheanum, which had burned to the ground less than a year before.

It was a bleak November afternoon, cloudy and damp with a premonition of rain in the air. The low overcast sky only increased the melancholy of the ruins. As I walked around the huge curved walls I came upon a deep-set opening with a doorway through which I could enter. Somewhat hesitatingly I stole inside.

A dim expanse, all of concrete, curved into dimmer recesses and made immediately a mysterious although beautiful impression. There were supporting pillars and light fell through several arched triptycal windows. Rather than being eerie it gave a sense of welcome and protection. It might, I thought, have been an archaic grotto or medieval chapel of immense and modern dimensions. At the far end I came upon a wide staircase leading on either side in swinging curves to what had been the building above, and at the base of each banister, a unique form caught my eye. It was composed of three harmoniously interrelated curves sculptured in concrete. They seemed to startle the newcomer into erectness, to cause him to listen and be alert, and with a touch of graceful humor to invite him to ascend.

Thus encouraged, I did so, with a sense of awe, trying to imagine what it would be like were I to be mounting these steps into the great auditorium all of carven wood which less than a year before had towered there above with its great pillars and architraves. Instead my way was barred by rough planks and beams set up against intruders and the weather. Peering between them as best I could I was able to look out over a bleak gray expanse of what had been the wide slanting floor of the amphitheatre with the stage beyond. Charred by smoke, wet by rains, it was now a forlorn maze of twisted iron rods protruding from the concrete, with ashen debris and lumps of melted glass strewn here and there. All that was left after the flames had finished! All that was left of the labors of ten years – of what had been built and hand-carved by the toil and artistry of men and women of seventeen different nationalities, while round about, even within earshot, the rest of the world had been plunged in the savage conflict of the first World War.

Conceived by Rudolf Steiner and carried out according to his sculptured model, it had been an edifice of two interlocking domes of unequal size, painted with colorful frescoes and supported on enormous carved pillars, while from the surrounding walls through large triptycal windows of carven glass of many hues, shafts of varicolored light illumined the whole. Like the interior of a great violin, sounding not only with the tones of music and of the spoken word, but with color and form — so it had been described to me. And this was what was left — this silent gravestone! I held my breath. ...

Was this really all — its end? I asked myself. Or did it still hover there just out of reach of my wondering gaze? Did it continue to stand in some mysterious realm of reality, accessible to the heart, where it might still awaken, protect and inspire men with the language and music of its mighty breathing structure? For an instant it seemed to quiver there. Then the ruins before me stabbed my eyes once more with the stark certainty that for all physical senses at least it was gone — irrevocably. The loss struck through me and I groped my way down the staircase once more, out onto the chill autumn hillside.

This building, I realized, was to have been a home of all the arts, the drama, in particular, in its highest form and meaning; for in it the great dramas of the past and of our own time were to have been performed. It was to have been a cultural home for all who sought spiritual insight, of whatever land or race. For above all, it was created to be a center from which a new, clearly founded knowledge of the spirit in our time might flow. And now — in view of these ruins?

What now of those creative impulses which had conceived it and brought it into existence with the help of the hands and hearts of innumerable people, and what of the knowledge it was to have served? These, it was clear to me, could not perish. They would manifest themselves again and again with ever renewed strength and healing. Yet at what inner and outer cost! And, in fact, even now in the face of this tragedy, plans were already in the air to erect on this very site a new building; a structure – actually quite different from the first — which today crowns the Dornach hill.

As I walked along, I became aware of a figure to my left climbing the hill to the Schreinerei. By the extraordinary carriage of the head and shoulders I recognized immediately that it was Rudolf Steiner. He appeared now more worn, even frailer, despite his heavy coat, yet he moved like a mountain climber whose fatigue is overcome by the freshness of the high places where he is at home.

What must he experience as he passed these ruins? ...

As I turned from their bleakness to watch him once more, there stood before my mind above all else a deep awareness of the unshakable trust and confidence in the power of good that lived in him, despite every adversity, and which he showed toward others even in his smallest deeds.

Finally, as he approached the entrance of the low weather-beaten building, someone opened the door and stepped out. He reached forward swiftly to clasp his hand and the two stood for a moment in conversation, Rudolf Steiner in a posture of complete selfless absorption.

Then in an instant he had vanished inside.

The Experience of the Christmas Foundation Meeting

Arvia MacKaye Ege

The Dornach hill in deep snow. Brilliant, starry nights. Cold, sparkling, clear days. The ruins of the Old Goetheanum – the gray, charred concrete lower structure, partially swept by drifts, a gaunt, mute reminder of the tragic night one year ago.

Behind the ruins and just above them on the hill, the low wooden barracks of the Schreinerei, the carpentry shop. Here during the days prior to the Christmas Conference, intense activity had been going on. The walls of the small auditorium situated in part of this building were being ripped out on two sides to open the hall toward the adjoining outer workshops. In this way it was hoped that many people – some coming from distant parts of the world – who had sent word that they were arriving for the Conference, would be able to see and, in any case, to hear. No one had anticipated such a large number. There was an atmosphere of intense expectations and preparation.

Then overnight people began to arrive. On the 24th, long processions came climbing up the hill through the snow, past the ruins, along the winding paths that mount steeply from the valley below. All converged upon this small weather-beaten door of the carpentry shop. Inside, the auditorium and adjoining workshops gradually became packed to overflowing as the people streamed in. Tightly placed chairs filled every bit of available floor space, the stage as well. People sat upon piles of planks in the background, on workbenches and anything they could find. It was impossible to heat the whole enlarged space adequately in the bitter cold, and especially out in the farther areas people sat wrapped in heavy overcoats and blankets. Young people were asked to give their seats to the arriving visitors, so many of us stood along the walls at the rear, or perched upon window ledges. Finding myself near a big machine for sawing lumber, I eagerly clambered up onto it and found myself a somewhat precarious seat on a small metal slab. From it, I was fortunate enough to be able to look out over the heads of the assembled people to the small speaker's stand placed at the far end of the auditorium from which Rudolf Steiner was to speak. This perch, being suitable only for a young climber, I was fortunately able to keep throughout the Conference.

A sense of profound earnestness, of almost breathless expectation and high festivity pervaded the gathering. There seemed to be so much going on in the way of last-minute preparations. Then at 10 A.M. Rudolf Steiner stepped to the podium.

The calm, moving dignity of his frail form, clad in black, against the blue curtains, the power and erect carriage of his head, the profound kindness and gravity of his features – the unforgettable depths of his gaze – rise once more in memory. For a long moment he stood silent, as was his custom before he spoke — an enormous quiet surrounding him. This his deep voice sounded, and with a few simple impressive words he pronounced the opening of the Christmas Conference, welcoming all who were present.

He spoke first of all, of the special significance of the fact, which should not be forgotten, that the Goetheanum and the center of the Society had been established upon Swiss soil. And with warm words he now asked Albert Steffen, "our dear and honored friend," to be the first speaker. Herr Steffen, the Swiss poet, then spoke on "The History and Destiny of the Goetheanum," giving, as a sort of prologue to the Conference, a revealing picture of the outer and inner reality of that great building with its high columns, carved capitals and architraves and colored windows, which had so recently passed through fire.

Then, at 11:15, Rudolf Steiner gave the opening address for the foundation of the Society in a new form, which he began with these words:[36]

> "We begin our Christmas meeting for the foundation of the Anthroposophical Society in a new form in the presence of a sharp contrast. We have had to invite you here, my dear friends, to a heap of ruins! These ruins are in many ways a symbol not only for the outer

aspects of our work and striving in the world – but they are symptomatic today for world conditions at large. (How ever more deeply true these words have become after fifty years! – A. M. E.)

You sit here in this provisional wooden structure which we have had to enlarge overnight in this poor house, this terribly meager home, in the midst of the ruins. Many of you have to suffer bitterly from the cold. But the more we can find our way into the mood and realization that all this outer world that surrounds us is Maya – illusion – the more we will be able to develop that strong, active mood which will be needed for the coming days.

… A revelation of the spirit has opened itself to humanity. Not out of any earthly, arbitrary action, but in obedience to a call which has sounded forth from the spiritual worlds, ... has the impulse for the Anthroposophical Movement flowed. This Anthroposophical Movement is not an earthly service. It is in its totality, right into all its details, a divine service. And we will find the right inner mood to approach it, if we behold it in its whole scope and entirety as such a divine service.

As such let us take it into our hearts at the beginning of this Christmas Conference. Let us write deeply into our hearts that this Anthroposophical Movement seeks to unite the soul of every single one who devotes himself to it with the primordial springs of all that is essentially human in the spiritual world; that it wants to guide the human being to that ultimate – and for him in the present stage of human evolution on earth – satisfying illumination which can clothe itself in the words: 'Yes, that am I as man, as spirit-willed man on earth, as God-willed man in the universe.'"

After these words Rudolf Steiner continued by giving the Statutes of the new Society and by appointing the members of the Vorstand (Executive Council). Who were these personalities? I will attempt to give a brief characterization of them, as I remember them at that time.

Rudolf Steiner, that unique human being I have already attempted to describe, who in assuming the presidency of the Society as its founder, selflessly took upon himself its future destiny together with the destinies of its members.

Albert Steffen, with impressive head and shoulders, eagle-like nose, unusually clear, quiet eyes and sensitive mouth, whom Rudolf Steiner designated as a co-founder of the Society – one who had been an anthroposophist before he was born – "the exceptional poet, whose presence in our midst we must look upon as the greatest good fortune."

Günther Wachsmuth, an eager alert scientist, then only in his early thirties, an extremely swift, energetic, executive young man – blond, lithe, like a young Hermes.

Frau Marie Steiner, that beautiful, so extraordinary and dramatic figure, about whom there was a spell of mystery, and without whose gifts and tremendous work the development of the artistic work and the early growth of the Society are unthinkable.

Frau Dr. Ita Wegman, a rather tall, active, warm, and in some ways seemingly plain woman, with strangely expressive and arresting eyes – a dedicated medical doctor – about whom there seemed to hover an atmosphere of something heroic as she strode along.

Frl. Dr. Vreede, a small compact person, whom one could immediately imagine – as Rudolf Steiner put it – crossing every *t* and dotting every *i* she ever wrote.

Today we ask, what was Rudolf Steiner preparing for the future through choosing these individualities as the founding Vorstand; how are we connected with them and interwoven in the great drama of the Society? For we become ever more deeply aware that this Society is the great mystery drama of our modern times – the Goetheanum, the mystery center of the new Christian mysteries.

Following this initial gathering and those recurring each morning, there were, in the afternoons throughout the Conference, performances either of the unforgettable Christmas Plays or of eurythmy, and in the evenings Rudolf Steiner's lectures on *World History in the Light of Anthroposophy*, a series deeply connected with the background of the Society. Each day was crowned by the outpouring of the spiritual substance and life which flowed from these lectures given in the evenings. Thus there was scarcely an unfilled moment throughout the nine days of the Conference.

Then, on the following day, Christmas morning , at 10 o'clock, Rudolf Steiner enacted the laying of the Foundation Stone of the General Anthroposophical Society. As he had laid the foundation stone for the Goetheanum building in the earth ten years earlier, he now laid the foundation stone of the new Society in the hearts of its members. Never had I seen him as he appeared then. There was a light in his eyes, a power and majesty about him which made him give the impression of having grown to a great size – an intensity and activity, united with a cosmic calm, which was breathtaking, indicative of what was to come.

He opened this event by giving three strong, incisive, measured raps with a gavel upon the speaker's stand, such as those given in the Temple in the Mystery Plays. It was as though the room became thronged with unseen spectators. Then as he spoke, speaking for the first time the words of the Christmas Foundation Mantram — Soul of Man — it was as though he spoke, in this little carpentry shop, not only to the whole earth but to the assembled heavens, as though he became like a sun, light outpouring, his voice like gold, a Michaelic fire infusing his words. Something poured forth of a magnitude, and in a realm of such awakened consciousness, on this Christmas morning, that can only be likened to a spiritual birth.

From my perch in the background, my heart cried out, because I realized that something so far beyond my grasp was taking place that it seemed as if it would burst. Then something gave way within me, and I drank in, like a great tide, all that followed, knowing that only in later incarnations would I approach any adequate realization of what was actually taking place.

His words sound over to us again today. *Out of these three: the Spirit of the Heights, the Christ-power encircling us, the creative Father-activity streaming out of the depths, we will in this moment form in our souls the twelve-sided Foundation Stone which we now sink deep into the ground of our souls.*

That morning Rudolf Steiner laid the dodecahedric Foundation Stone into the hearts of all anthroposophists. And from what transpired it was apparent that he did so as a mystery deed. We sense that this deed, while taking place here on the earth, was enacted on the highest spiritual plane, and as such was a deed that cannot pass away. It is there awaiting us always. And because it was enacted on that plane, it can multiply itself infinitely and become a reality in the heart of each one of us. Thus we are able today to begin to approach it as an archetypal seed sown in humanity — the seed of a free spiritual community of human beings.

Following this Christmas event, each morning throughout the Conference, Rudolf Steiner opened the meetings with the words of the Christmas mantram, dealing with its various rhythms. I remember so well how each day he wrote the verses on a blackboard set up for the purpose, for everyone to copy. The harmony and beauty of his writing always seemed to me like a starry script – it flowed with such grace, strength and balance.

And now I would like to try to describe a final picture, at the end of the Conference.

After all that had taken place – the amazing passage of the days, filled with a mood of highest festival and gravity, the deed consummated – would anyone, could anyone, say something in response? And then a figure arose, Herr Werbeck, and did what was in a way impossible, because no one was of course adequate to it. He thanked Rudolf Steiner. It was as though he were the spokesman for all the hearts of those who were there. And, oh, how grateful we were that someone had the courage to do it!

And then there followed a picture which is imprinted deep within me as something to be held apart and seldom touched, because it is like a window into a deep mystery. When Herr Werbeck had finished speaking, the frail but majestic figure of Rudolf Steiner bent down – and kissed him. And then, after a long moment, with a scarcely to be fathomed modesty and at the same time tenderness, turned the thanks from himself, directing the gaze of all instead, beyond the ruins, to the eternal Spirit of the Goetheanum, in whose name he had spoken, and in whose name he now accepted this thanks.

This picture is to me like a Mystery picture, through which we are allowed to glimpse a great sacrificial deed in the course of human history.

In concluding, perhaps I may recall the following words which Rudolf Steiner spoke during the final lecture, before ending with those timeless verses of the Christmas mantram, and which now sound again strongly in my memory.

"Through all that has transpired here, we will have understood in our hearts, as we pass these ruins, that in the future there will arise spiritual flames which will spring forth as true spiritual life from the re-arisen Goetheanum for the blessing of mankind – which will spring forth through our seal and through our devotion. The more we are filled with courage, my dear friends, as we leave this gathering – courage for the pursuit of all anthroposophical activity, the better we will have understood what has permeated these meetings like a hope-filled breath of the spirit throughout these days. … The voice admonishing to courage and through courage to awakening – that is what sounds for all anthroposophists in the life of present-day civilization."

Endnotes

1 For information about Steiner's upbringing see *Autobiography: Chapters in the Course of My Life*, Rudolf Steiner, Anthroposophic Press, Hudson, NY (1999); *Rudolf Steiner – Eine Chronik 1861-1925*, by Christoph Lindenberg, Verlag Freies Geistesleben, Stuttgart (1988); and *Self-Education: Autobiographical Reflections* 1861-1893, Rudolf Steiner, Mercury Press, Spring Valley, NY (1985) This autobiographical report was given by Steiner on February 4, 1913 in Berlin, during the General Assembly that marked the founding of the first Anthroposophical Society. There are also many biographies of Rudolf Steiner that speak of his early years, including *A Life for the Spirit: Rudolf Steiner in the Crosscurrents of Our Time* by Henry Barnes, Anthroposophic Press, Hudson, NY (1997).

2 *Correspondence and Documents, 1901-1925: Rudolf Steiner and Marie Steiner-von Sivers*, Rudolf Steiner Press, London, and Anthroposophic Press, New York (1988). p 264.

3 *Self-Education*, p 2

4 *ibid*, pp 5 – 8

5 A new compilation entitled *Working with the Dead* contains many of Rudolf Steiner's verses for the dead, as well as some of his comments on the relationship between the living and the dead, with particular attention to the death of children. Waldorf Early Childhood Association of N.A., Spring Valley, NY (2003). Available from WECAN at. 845.352.1690.

6 *Autobiography*, pp 46-47

7 *Correspondence and Documents*: Taken from "Notes by Rudolf Steiner Written for Edouard Schuré", p 10.

8 *Journal for Anthroposophy*, Number 34, Autumn 1981. "First Meeting with Rudolf Steiner," p 74.

9 *Music and Music-Making* by Bruno Walter was published by W.W. Norton & Co. in 1961, translated from the 1957 German publication. For additional information on Bruno Walter see http://www.andante.com/profiles/walter/index.cfm (retrieved 2.13.05).
The opening paragraph describes Walter in this way: "Bruno Walter (1876-1962) was one of the leading conductors of the first half of the 20th century. A close friend of Gustav Mahler, Walter gave the world-premiere performances of two cornerstones of the symphonic repertoire: Mahler's *Ninth Symphony* and *Das Lied von der Erde*. His long tenures in Vienna,

Munich, Berlin, and Leipzig established Walter as one of the most important interpreters of his day, especially in the field of Austro-German repertoire. His Jewish heritage, however, inevitably led to his expulsion from Germany in 1933 and from Austria in 1938. He eventually settled in the United States, where he worked regularly with the Metropolitan Opera, the New York Philharmonic, the Los Angeles Philharmonic, and the San Francisco Symphony. In the late 1950s he made a number of stereo recordings with the Columbia Symphony Orchestra, for which he is most widely remembered. In his final years, encouraged by his friend Delia Reinhardt, he developed a deep interest in the ideas of Rudolf Steiner.

10 Published as *The Philosophy of Civilization: Part I, The Decay and the Restoration of Civilization; Part II, Civilization and Ethics*. By Albert Schweitzer. Edited by C.T. Campion, Prometheus Books, Amherst, NY. Publication date unknown.

11 In a manuscript signed by Belyi around 1926, he refers to his devotion to Soloviev (1853-1900) in this way: "After Soloviev died I ended up like an orphan, totally uncared-for." See www.Bibliopoly.com for text of manuscript. (retrieved 9.14.03)

12 Translated into English from *Verwandlung des Lebens* (Transforming of Life) by Andrei Belyi. Translated from the Russian into German by Swetlana Geier and published by Zbinden Verlag, Basel, Switzerland. The sections included in this volume have been translated into English by Maria St. Goar and Sonia Tomara Clark.

13 Belyi is referring to Steiner's terms for the three higher aspects of the human being's spiritual nature: *Manas* or Spirit Self, *Budhi* or Life Spirit, and *Atman* or Spirit Man. The latter is the highest of the three. Rudolf Steiner used these Sanskrit terms during his time with the Theosophical Society and when he published his early editions of *Theosophy*, one of his most basic books, which first appeared in 1904. For more details, see *Theosophy*, page 54 of the 1994 edition published by Anthroposophic Press.

14 Reference to Friedrich Nietzsche's *Froehliche Wissenschaft*, 1882.

15 As Marie Steiner was born in Russia, Belyi uses her Russian patronymic. In Russia a person is respectfully referred to by first name and second name which is the father's first name. Yakovlevna means daughter of Yakov.

16 Belyi's wife, Assia Turgenieff (also spelled Assya Tourguenieff). Her full name was Anna Alekseyeva Turgenyeva-Bugayevna.

17 Mieta Waller, later Mrs. Scott Pyle.

18 This passage refers to the Anthroposophical Society as it existed before Rudolf Steiner gave it a new form and became its leader at the Christmas Foundation Meeting in 1923.

19 Refers to a certain type of fanatical, emotional Steiner-follower, who complicated matters wherever they appeared. The "Uncles" ("Onkel") were the male counterparts.

20 A different conception is put forth in *The Christmas Foundation: Beginning of a New Cosmic Age* by Rudolf Grosse, SteinerBooks, Hudson, NY. Belyi was in Russia at the time of the refounding of the Society and formed his impressions from a distance. Many individuals see the refounded Anthroposophical Society as a direct continuation of Rudolf Steiner's work and mission.

21 It would be far more accurate to speak of Steiner's wish to transform the state through the Threefold Social Order rather than to abolish it.

22 From *Erinnerungen an Rudolf Steiner*, Verlag Freies Geistesleben (Stuttgart). Translated by Christy Barnes. An excerpt from the book appeared in the *Journal for Anthroposophy*, Number 26, Autumn 1977.

23 He is probably referring to the Oberufer plays, plays from the Middle Ages found on an island in the Danube, and which are frequently performed in Waldorf schools.

24 Pavel Motschalov, 1800 – 1848, famous Russian actor.

25 Starets has several meanings but refers here to the holy men of Russia.

26 Nikish, Arthur, 1855-1922; Hungarian conductor.

27 A foothill behind the Goetheanum.

28 The building where the glass windows for the Goetheanum were carved.

29 Stanislav Wyspianski. 1869-1907; Polish dramatist, painter and graphic artist, a representative of a Polish trend of art called "Decadence."

30 The German word "ich" means I, but it is also related to J. Ch., *Jesus Christus*.

31 In German there is a play on words here illustrating the point. The selfish "owner" (innkeeper is *Wirt* in German) and the unselfish shepherd (*Hirt* in German, rhyming with *Wirt*) who gives of himself.

32 Reminiscences by Nathalie Turgenieff-Pozzo, sister of Assia Turgenieff.

33 This is the building on the hilltop with the Goetheanum, then owned by

Dr. Grosheintz, a dentist who donated the land for the Goetheanum. The building now houses the Rudolf Steiner Verlag (Press), which publishes Rudolf Steiner's books and lectures, and houses an archive containing some of his personal materials, including his library. For more information see http://www.rudolf-steiner.com/

34 Lisa Monges added a footnote: This is an authentic memory. One must, however, be careful how one interprets such a remark and consider that there are many aspects of the human individuality, especially in those most spiritually active.

35 Nancy Poer, working out of Anthroposophy, has helped many individuals and their families at the time of death. She writes in her book, *Living into Dying*, that special signs of nature often appear in relation to a person's death. She gives wonderful examples, including the role of birds in this regard (pp 152-154). Available from Rudolf Steiner College Bookstore at 916. 961.8729 or bookstore@steinercollege.edu.

36 For a complete report of the Christmas Foundation Conference in English see *The Christmas Conference* by Rudolf Steiner. Anthroposophic Press (1990).

Editor's Note: These endnotes are a compilation of those found in the original *Journals* with some modifications and additions.

Moving?

Please notify us six weeks before you move to ensure that you receive your next *Journal*.

Name _____

Old Address:

Address _____
City/State/Postal Code _____

New Address:

Address _____
City/State/Postal Code _____

Send to: *Journal For Anthroposophy*
             1923 Geddes Ave., Ann Arbor, MI 48104

ANTHROPOSOPHY

Yes, I would like to subscribe / resubscribe.

I enclose payment of __ $22 USA, __ $25 Canada,
__ $27 overseas for a one year (2 issue) subscription.

Name _____

Address _____

City/State/Postal Code _____

Send to: *Journal For Anthroposophy*
             1923 Geddes Ave., Ann Arbor, MI 48104

"CLASSIC" SELECTIONS FROM
THE JOURNAL FOR ANTHROPOSOPHY

Four very special issues, comprised of outstanding "classic" articles selected from the *Journal for Anthroposophy* are planned to appear over the next two years starting in October 2005. Each issue will focus on a specific theme and be edited by a different individual who is responsible for selecting articles from as far back as the 1960's and writing the introduction to the volume.

Robert McDermott is the General Editor of the "Classics" series. Other editors include: Joan Almon, Kate Farrell, Arthur Zajonc, and Douglas Sloan.

Existing or new subscribers will receive the "Classic" editions as a part of their subscription. If you live in the U.S., one-year (two issue) subscriptions to the *Journal for Anthroposophy* are $22.00 / year; mailed to Canada $25.00; mailed overseas $27.00

These special editions will likely become sought-after because of their unique content. Every effort is being made to make them available as widely as possible. They will be offered to bookstores on a quantity basis. And, SteinerBooks has agreed to offer them through their catalog.

It's not too early to begin planning on sending a copy as a gift for Christmas.

The First In The "Classic" Series – *Meeting Rudolf Steiner*

Robert McDermott, PhD, was president and is currently professor of philosophy and religion at the California Institute of Integral Studies. He was formerly professor and chair of the department of philosophy at Baruch College, CUNY. His publications include *Radhakrishnan*, *The Essential Aurobindo*, and *The Essential Steiner*.

Joan Almon is an internationally known educator, former Chair of the Waldorf Early Childhood Association, past-President of the Waldorf Kindergarten Association, Coordinator the Alliance For Childhood, a nonprofit partnership of educators, health professionals and other advocates for children; Co-General Secretary of the Anthroposophical Society in America, and former editor of its *News For Members*.